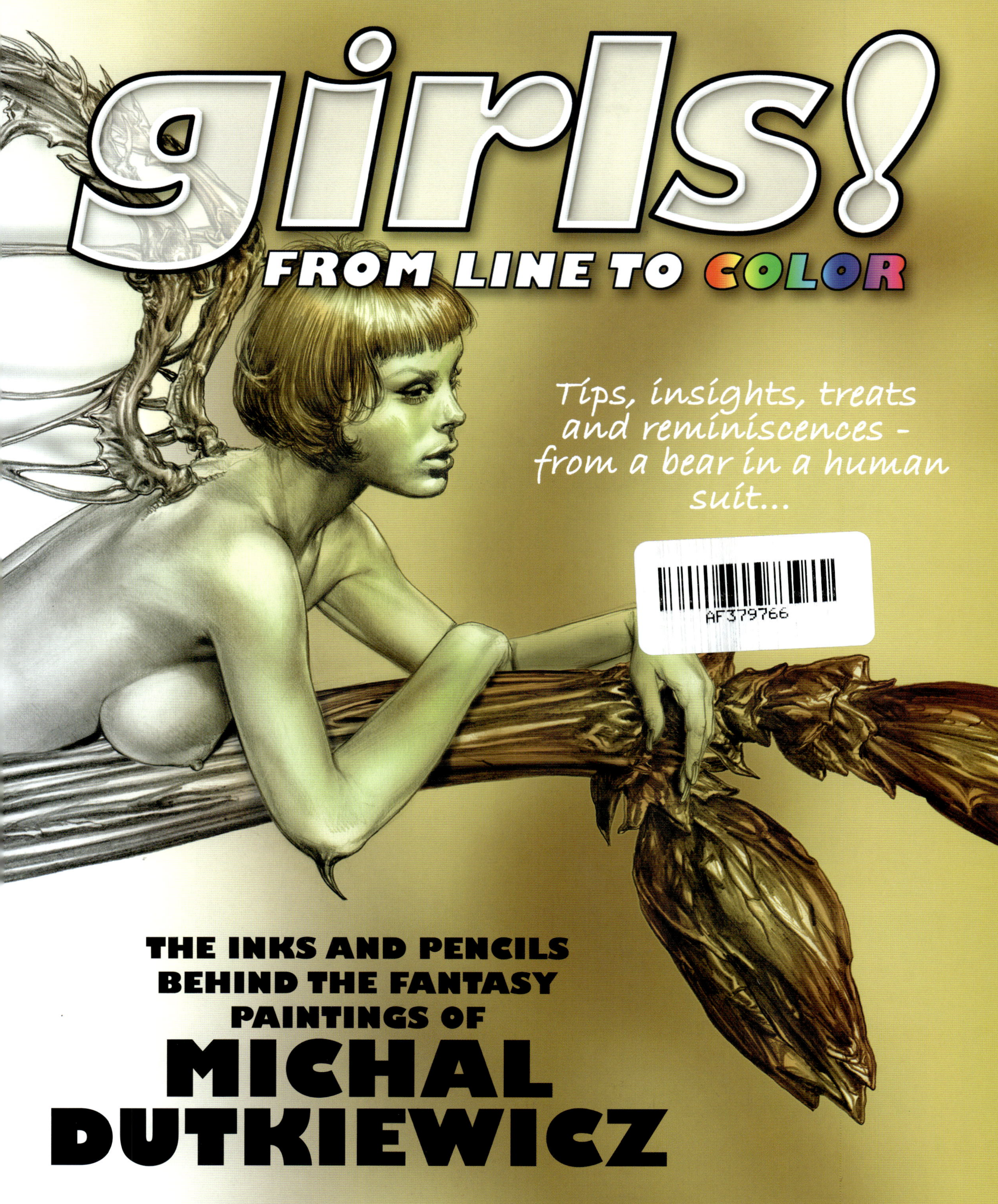

girls!
FROM LINE TO COLOR
Tips, insights, treats and reminiscences - from a bear in a human suit...
THE INKS AND PENCILS BEHIND THE FANTASY PAINTINGS OF
MICHAL DUTKIEWICZ
AN SQP PRESENTATION

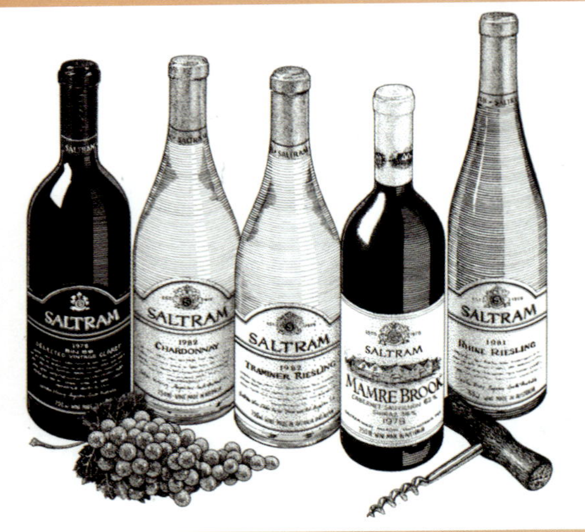

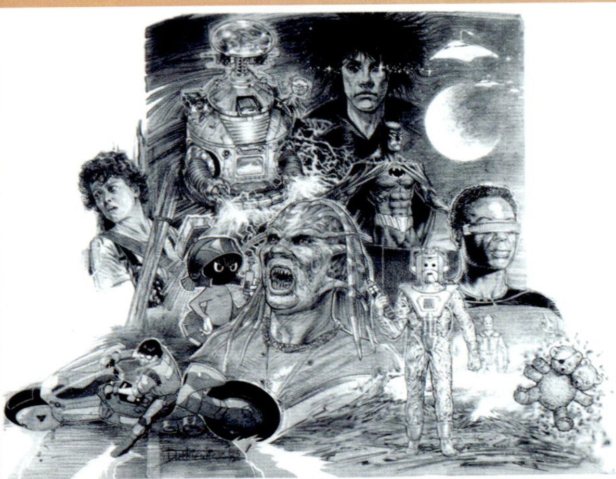

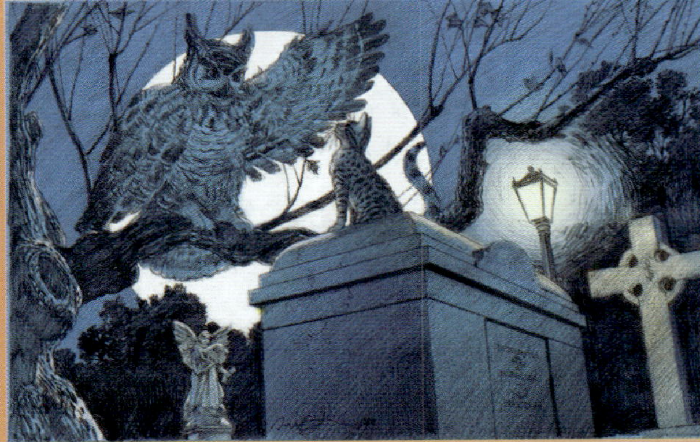

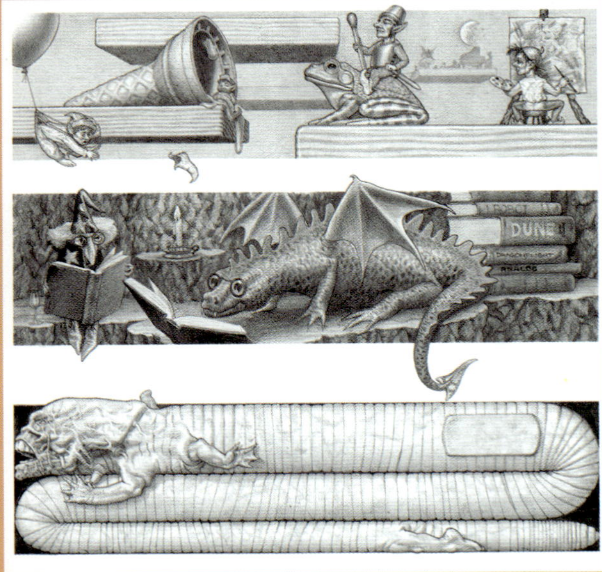

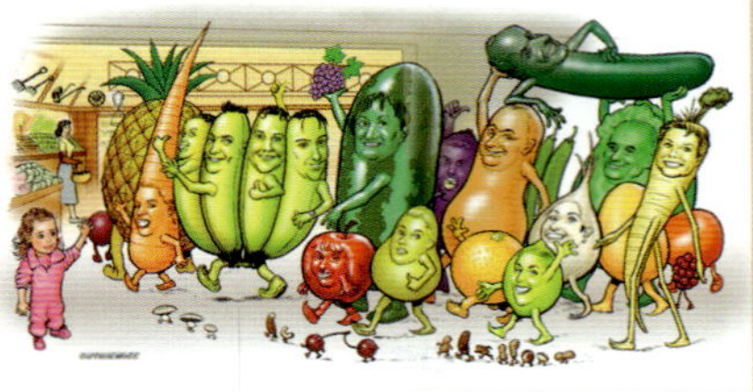

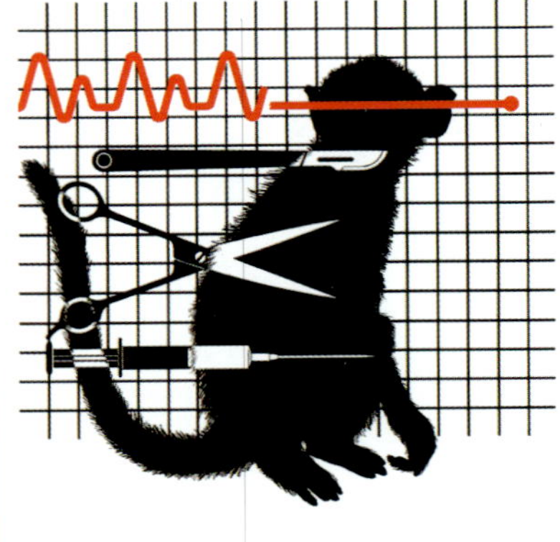

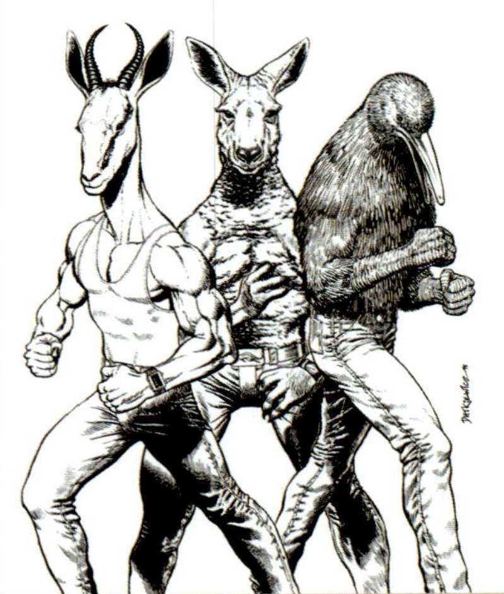

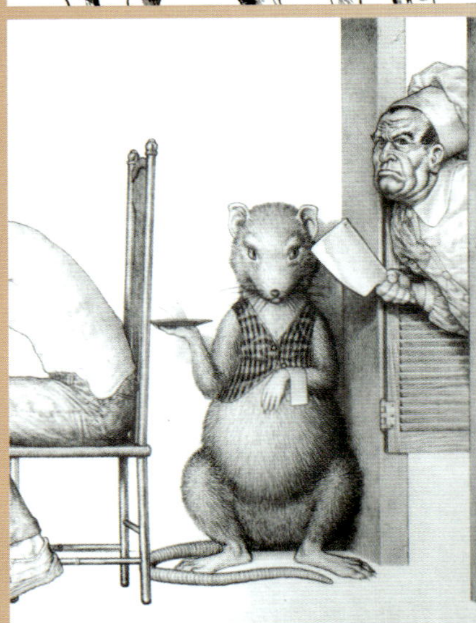

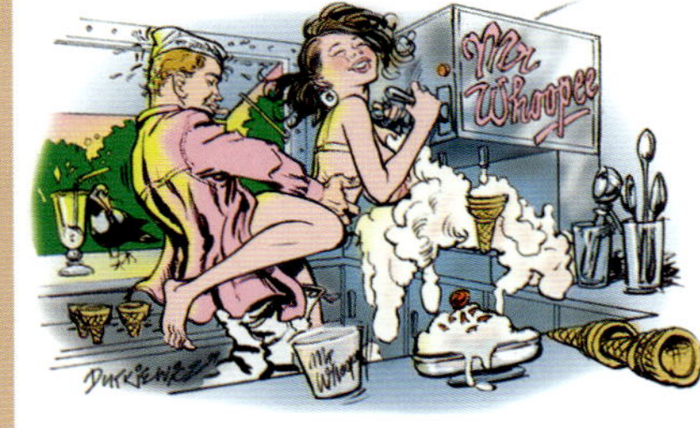

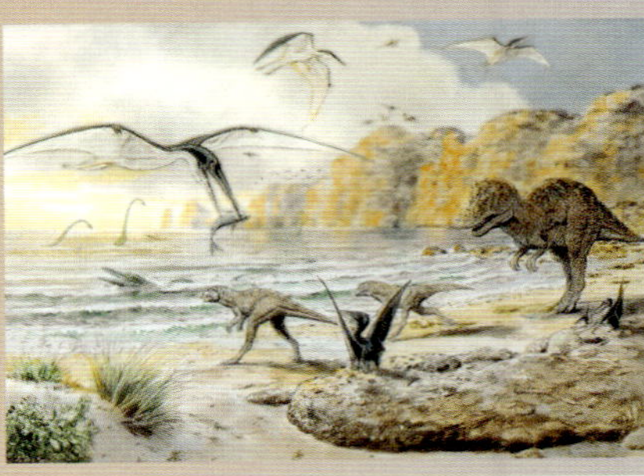

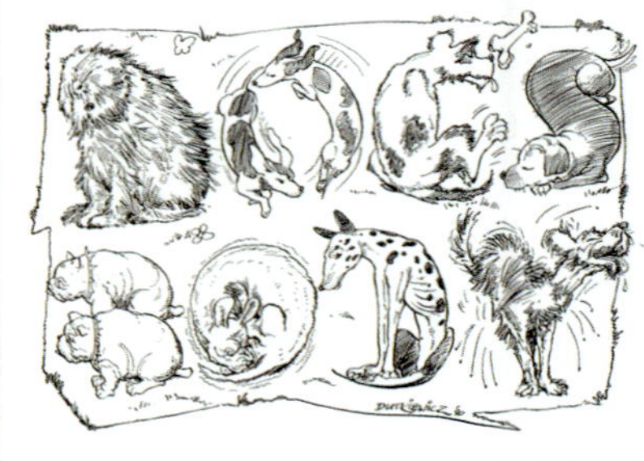

On this double-page introductory spread I have featured a few of my pieces. Some are private, such as the pages from my own comics: top right, *Platinum*, and bottom right, *Verity Aloeha*.
Some of this work is unpaid, done for friends, and has never been printed before.
The small Dinosaur color scene above is gouache over pencils, but all other color works here are early exercises in digital color. The rest are either pen, pastel, pencil or brush.

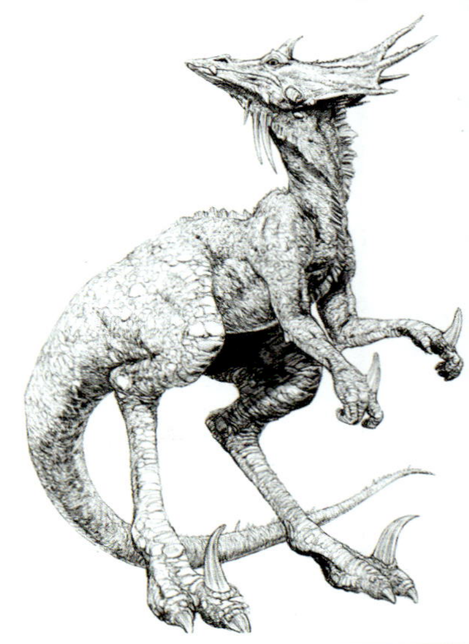

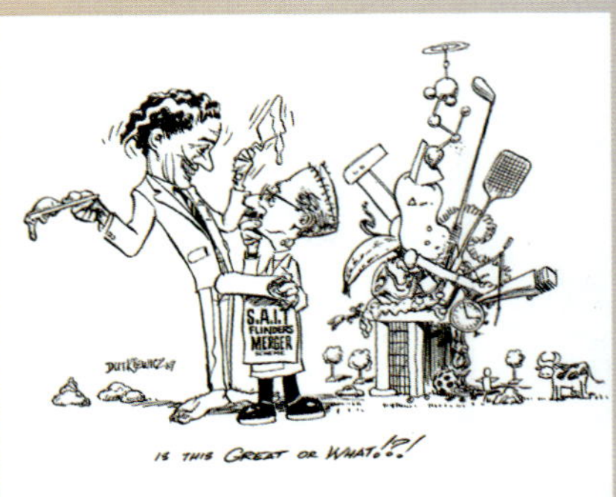

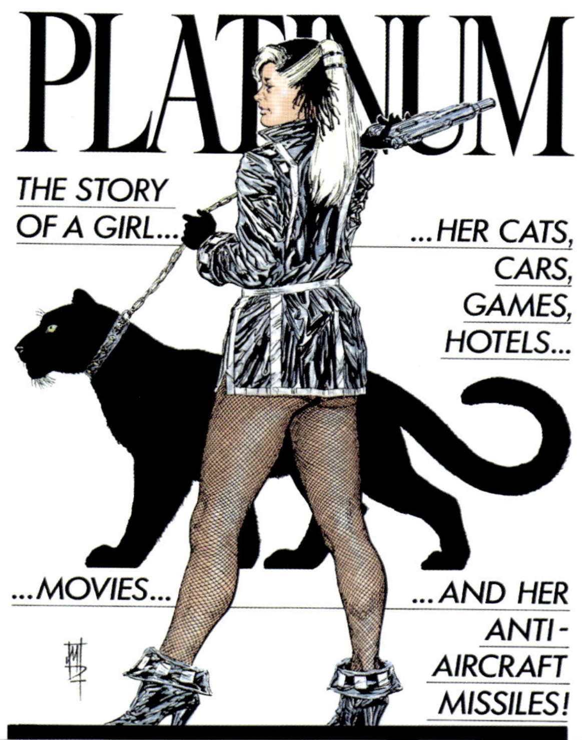

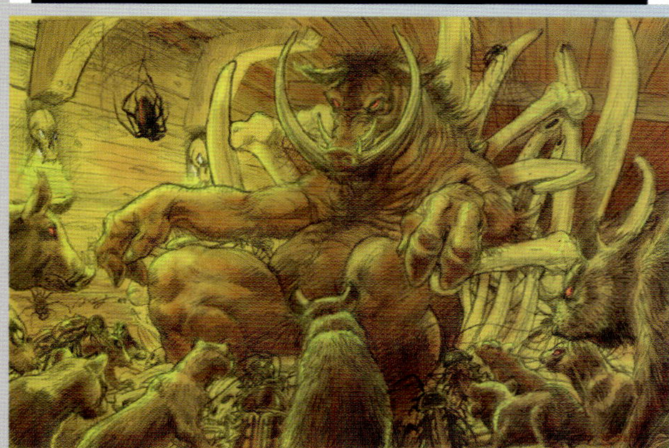

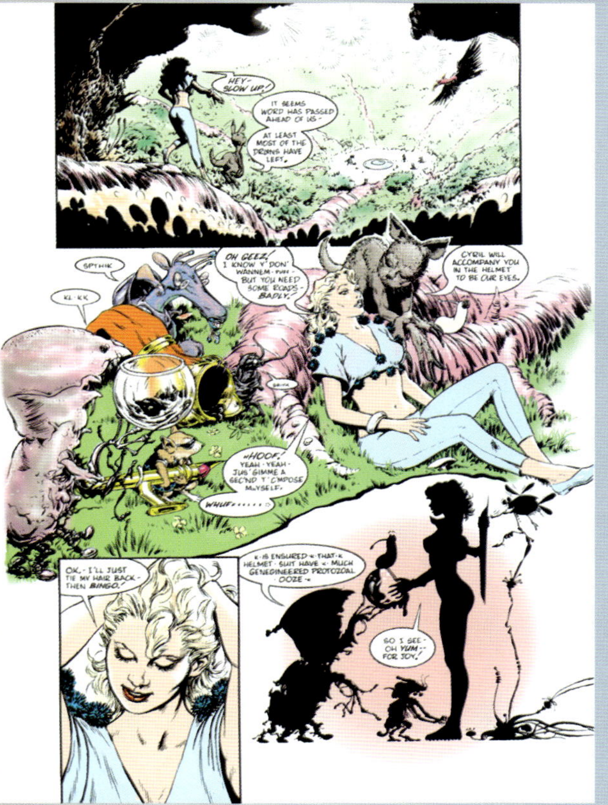

FOREWORD

Over the years that I have been an artist/illustrator, I've dabbled in many areas, mediums and styles. I've used pencils, oil paints, gouache, collage, frottage, scraperboard, airbrush, cut-outs, computers, ink, brushes, pens, and so on. I've painted houses, stage scenery, built model sets for miniature photography, painted abstract and surrealist and optical art. I've been asked to do the widest range of commercial imagery - porn, hardware catalogues, political and editorial cartoons, menu covers, business cards, labels and letterheads, calendars, displays of biological, historical and palaeontological visualizations for museums, health brochures and CD Roms, music and movie posters and film and TV concept work, children's' books, comic books and most fun of all - Pin-Up Girls.

I have worked on a wide variety of surfaces, but by far the biggest revelations in my life, in terms of art techniques and materials, paradoxically, are light years apart in terms of techniques required for their mastery, their technologies and their applications. They are: Pencils and Computers!

From my first attempts, some seven years ago, to scan in and digitally color my images, I found I was perplexed and fascinated about how to exploit the rich and tantalizing possibilities of both media. I wanted not only to give both free rein, but also to try to blend the two, aesthetically if not seamlessly. Although this book is more personal than technical in emphasis, I sincerely hope that you will find it useful and enjoyable.

ATB - M

INTRODUCTION

Illustration is hard to master, and there have been many Masters. I don't regard myself as an expert, and all I can show you is some of my stumblings and victories. Some of you might remember my comic book work on Batman Forever and Lost In Space, but now I primarily concentrate on book illustration and concept illustration.

If you seek to improve your work - don't be afraid of being a little self-critical...

At Right - this was based on
one of a series of four quick, but
well-thought-out sketch-briefs
I had requested from Peter
Broelman, a noted Australian
cartoonist with a growing
international reputation.
I had no idea at the time of the
requirements of the job.
For instance, notice that
I drew the Pirate Lass with
pants on and a peasant blouse...

Not only did the brief lend itself
to the exploitation of eye-
grabbing shapes, but I also had
to restrain myself from going wild
on textures - to lighten the mood
of the piece and focus on the key
ingredients and actions.

I had not realized, until the
year 1999, exactly how important
computers had become to both
Artists/Illustrators and Editors/
Publishers alike.

Below - the final color version of
0001 - A Parrot Spurned.

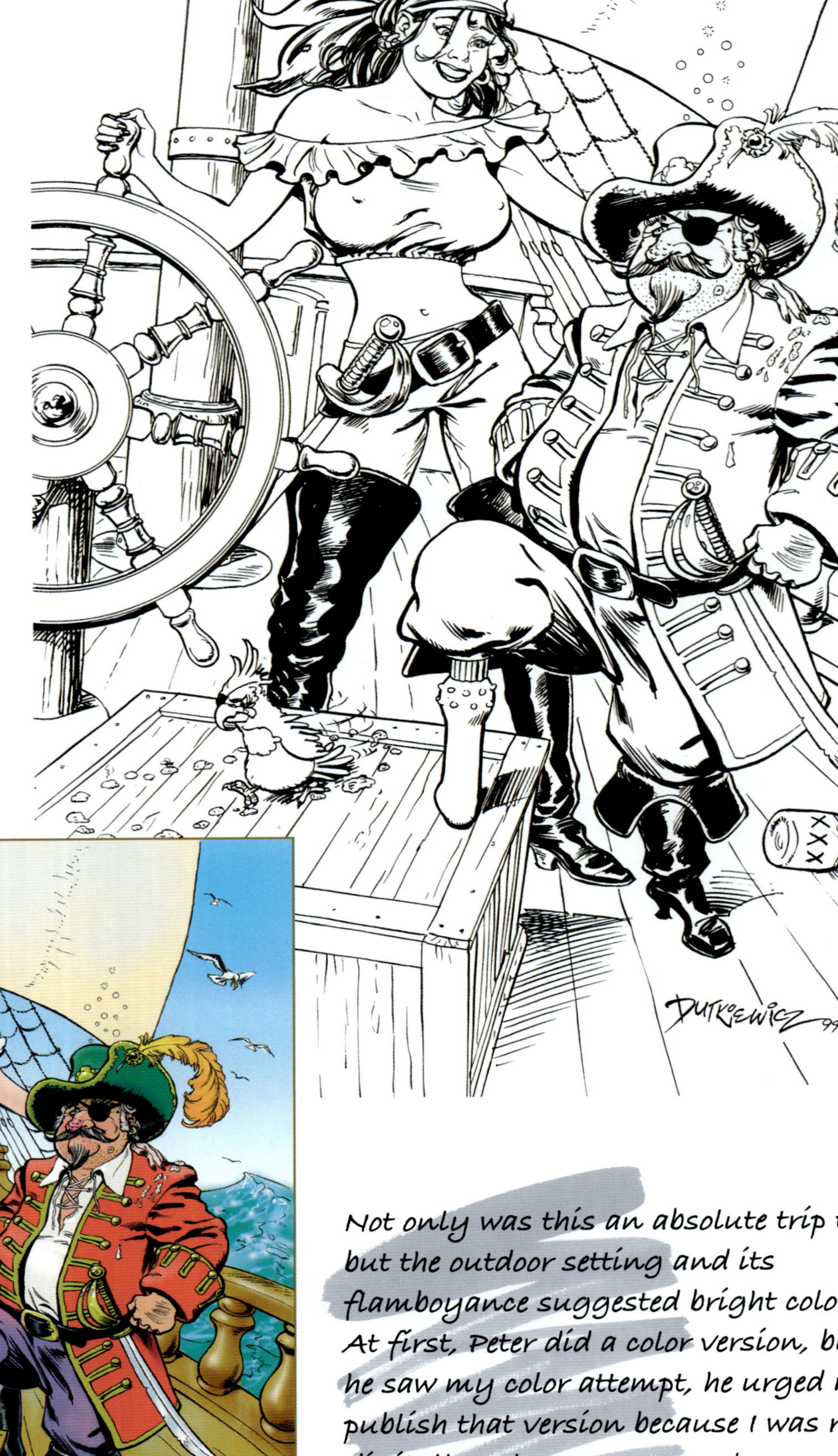

Not only was this an absolute trip to draw,
but the outdoor setting and its
flamboyance suggested bright colors.
At first, Peter did a color version, but when
he saw my color attempt, he urged me to
publish that version because I was ready to
digitally color my own work.

These two pieces were colored
within a month or two of my getting
my first computer. At the time I thought
16 gigabytes of hard drive space was huge,
but it filled up very quickly with my many
experiments with digital painting and
texture-making - many of these I still
use today...

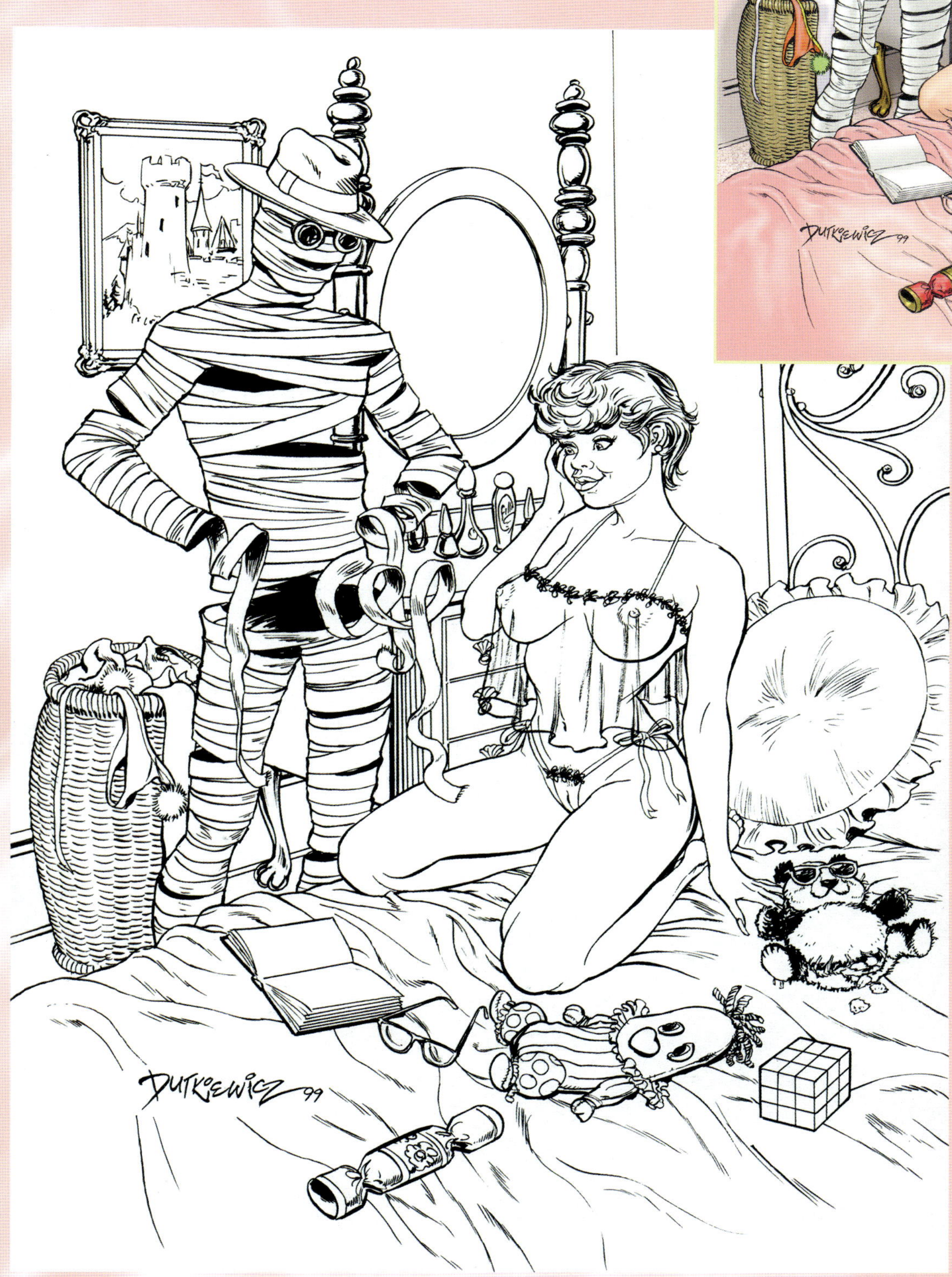

At Left -
0002 - Invisible Manhood -
once again, Peter's gag writing
was tops.

I felt the need to restrain myself
from over-doing the Photoshop
rendering. I used a dry brush,
impastoish effect created with
filters to embellish the picture
on the wall.

Both the works on these two
pages are old-school, in that I
didn't composite or alter the
images in Photoshop on the
Line Art layer - which,
incidentally, I usually keep on
the Multiply Layer Blending
Mode - with colors on Normal
Layer Blending Mode on a
Layer underneath.

I had a hard time explaining to
my brother, three sisters
and mother what my new job
entailed. Out of all of
them, it was my mother who
blew me away by really
enjoying a lot of the pieces.

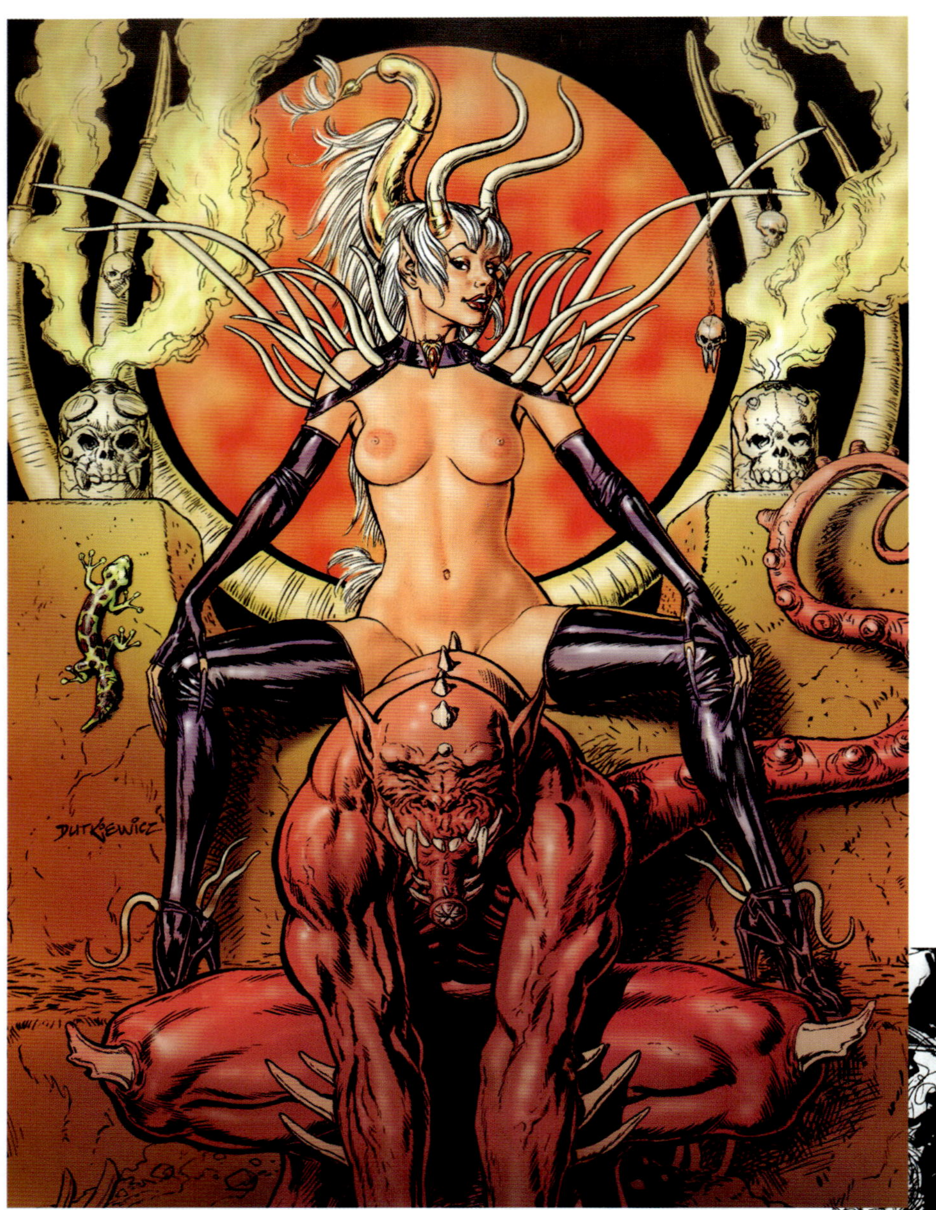

Above - the finished art is cropped to the final shape and size for the Pin-Up **0003-Horny Devil**. This picture is from my first book of Pin-Ups, still available from SQP.

I drew this sketch in a cappuccino bar, across the road from a beautiful parkland setting. My hometown is very beautiful and has quite a reputation for cafes...

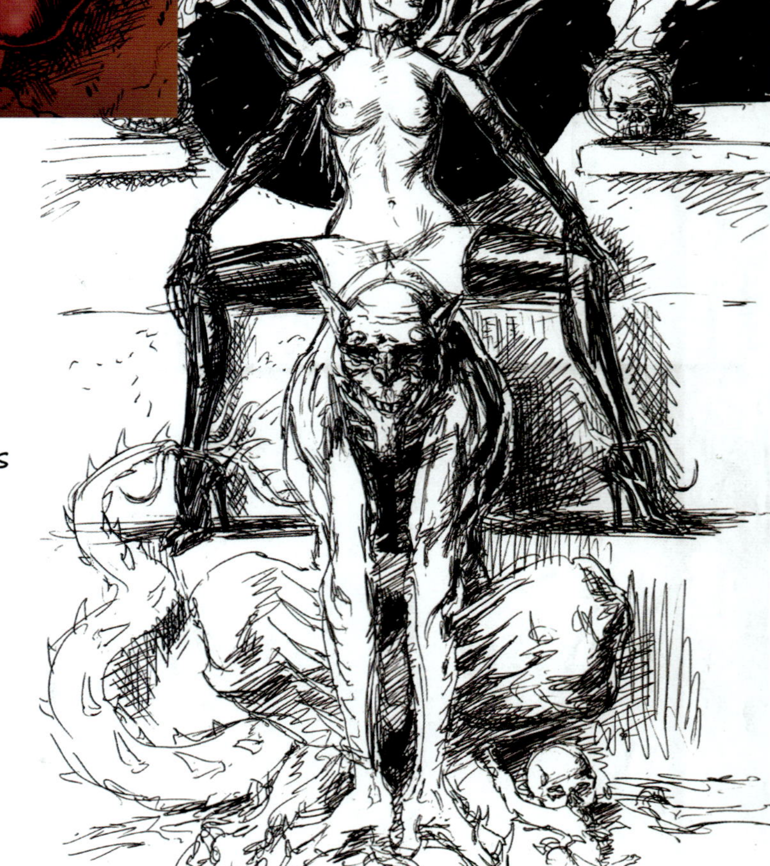

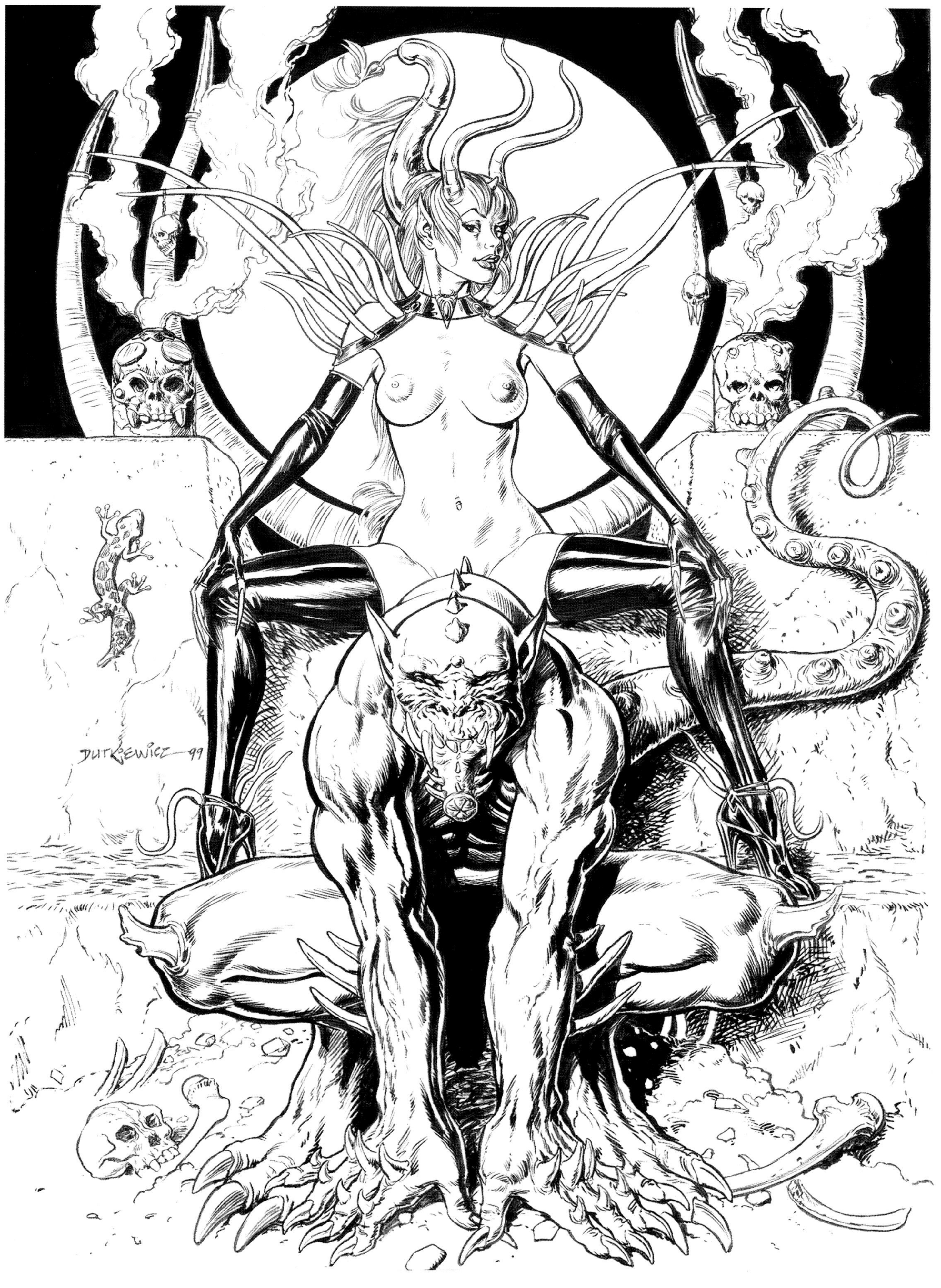

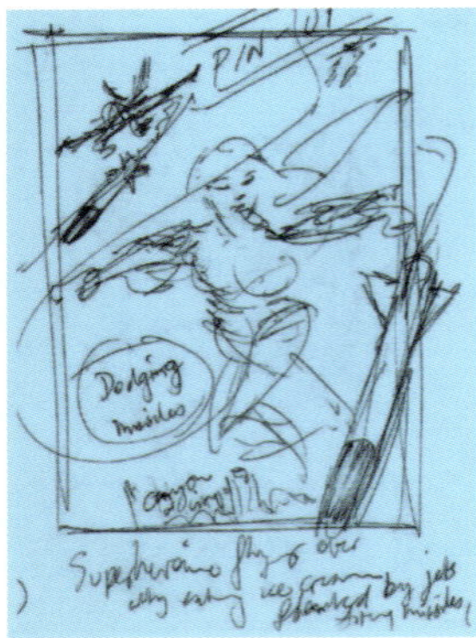

Above - this is the first sketch for
0006-Girl Power.
It's just an instinct and some
barely-there notes...

At Right - a bit of a spot-the-difference.
You should be able to see several
differences in these - there is no prize.

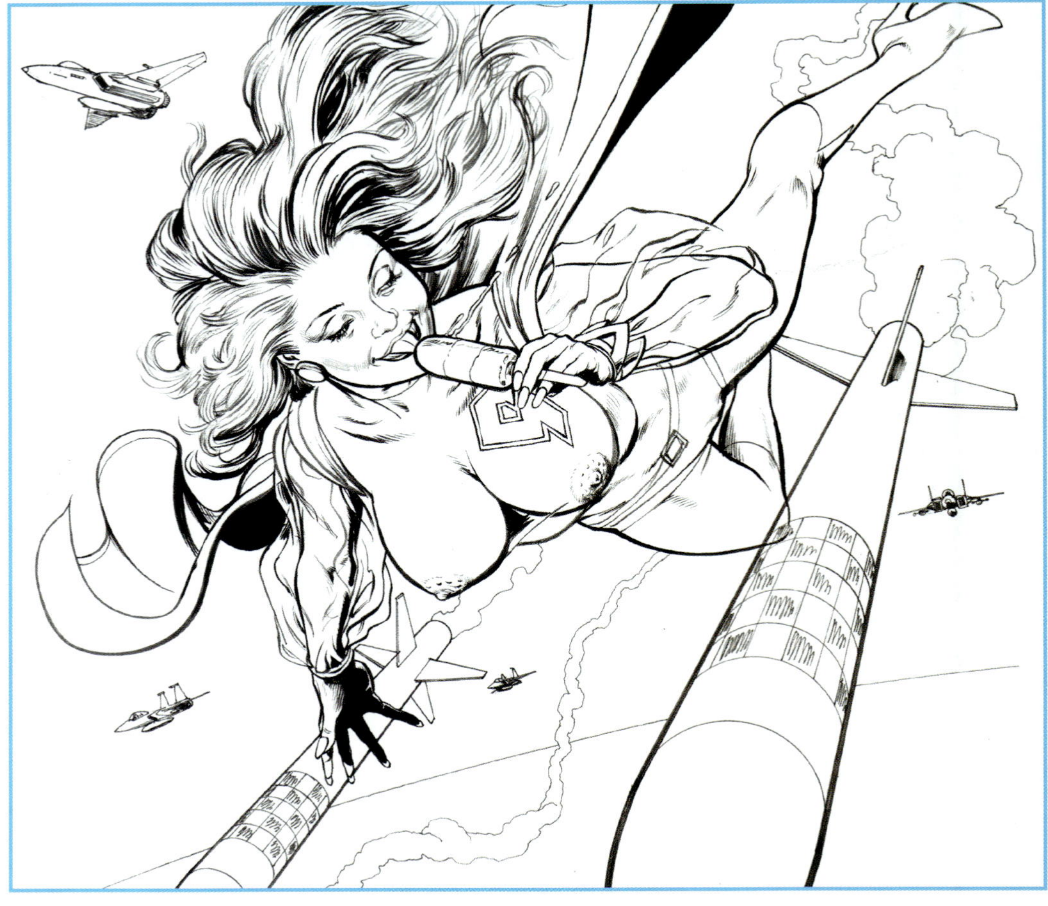

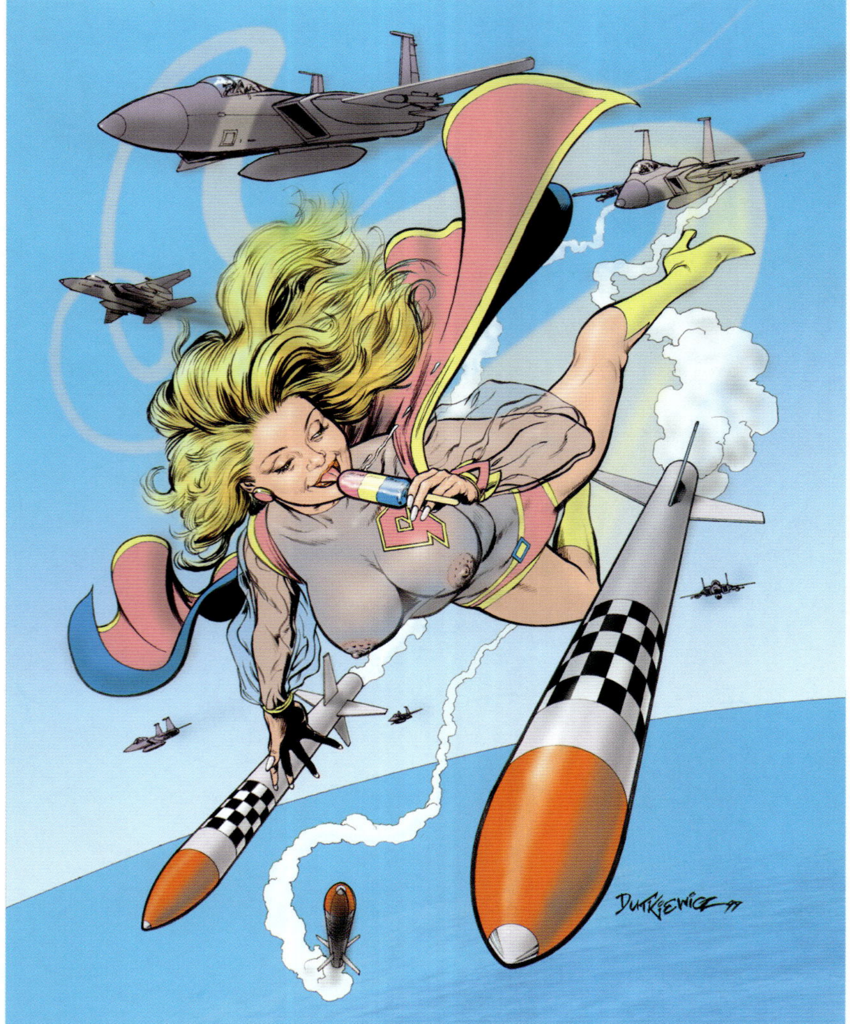

I was spoiled by the amount of creative freedom in my weekly Pin-Up gig. I often said I felt a little like Scheherazade - in that all my Editorial brief stated was that I had to come up with an entertaining picture every time...

Left - this is the final art for **0006-Girl Power**. When I first started doing the Minxes page I wrote pages of single-sentence or paragraph outlines for Pin-Up ideas. Later on the ideas often seemed more organic in origin.

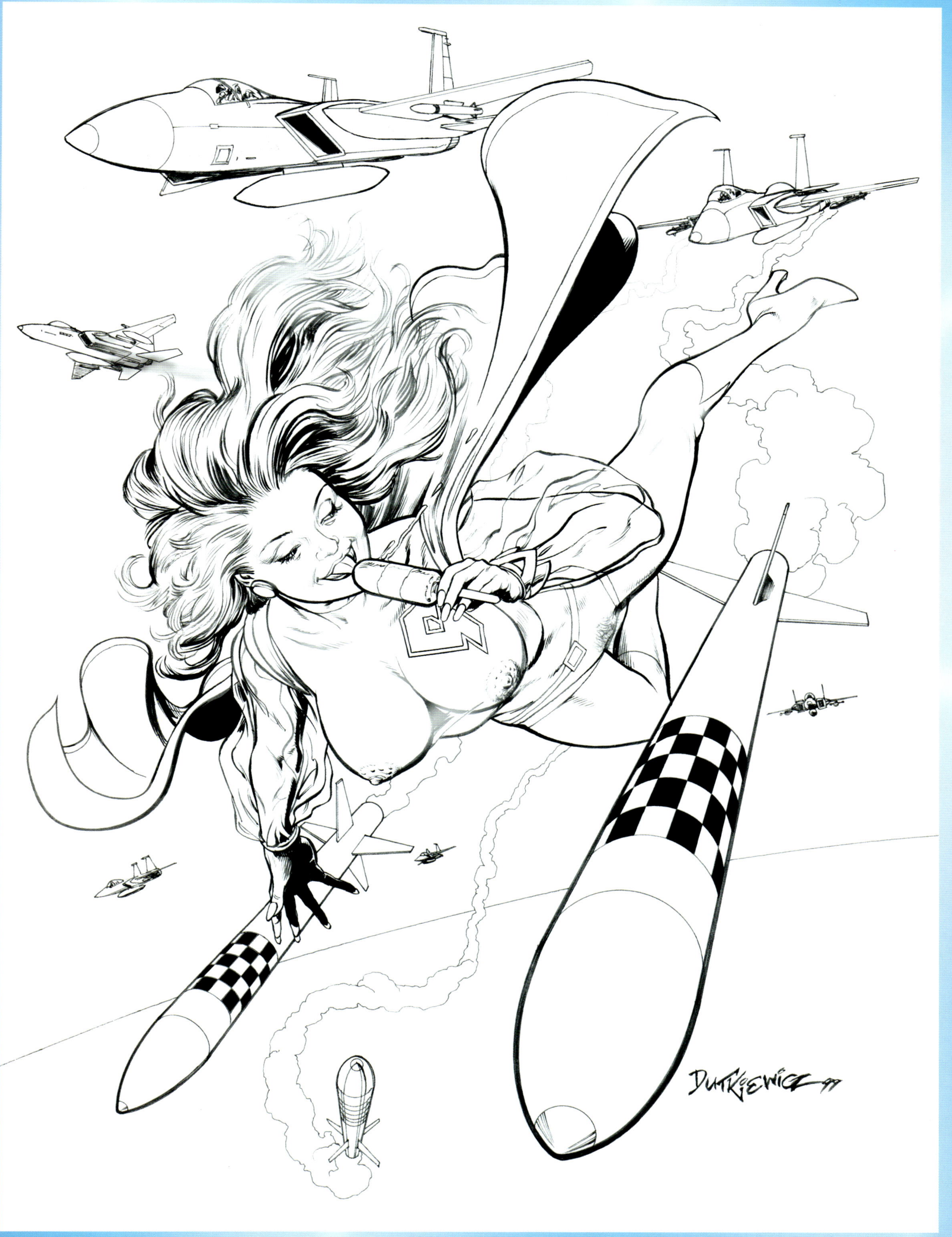

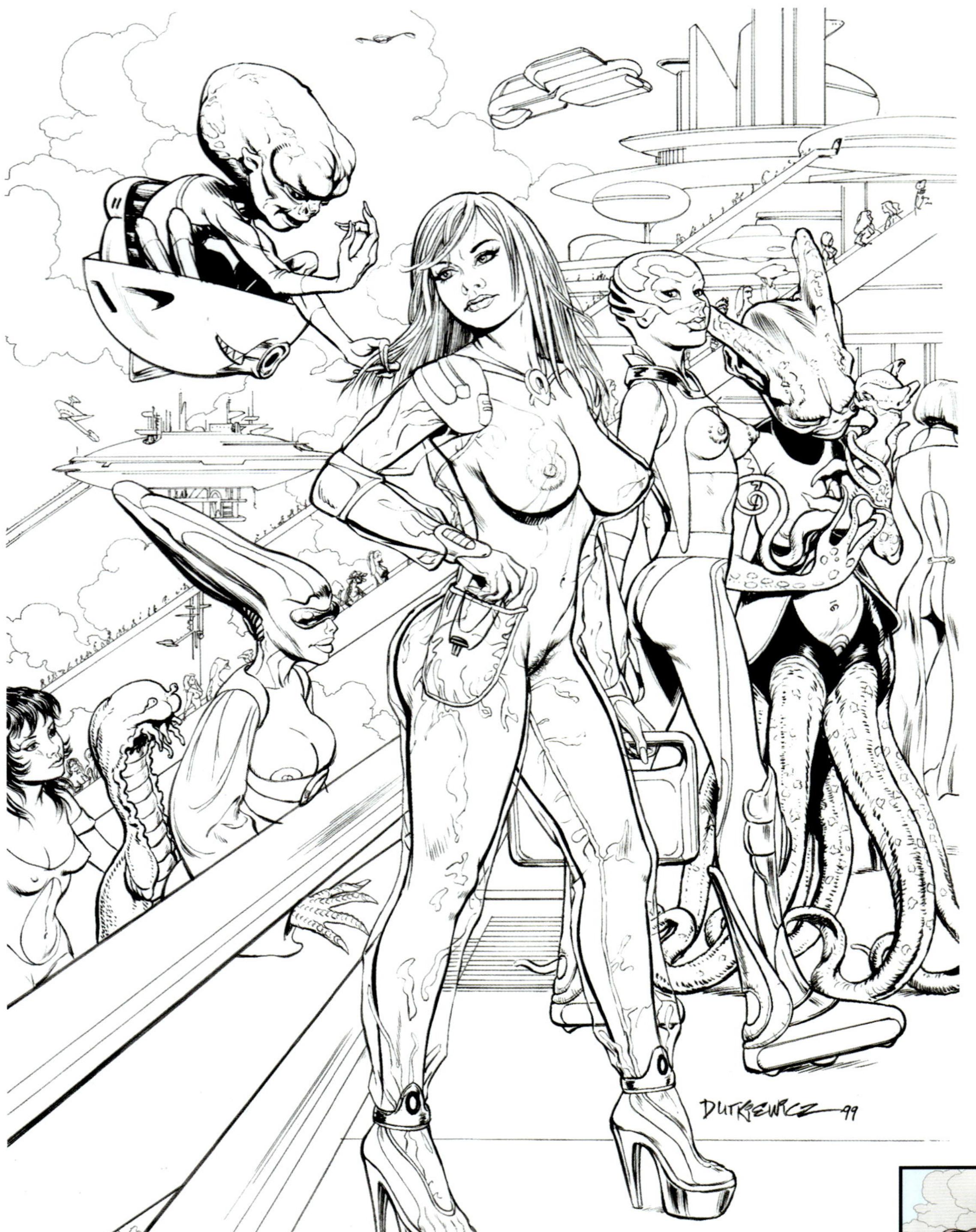

At Left - the finished inks for **0004-Chat Up Line**. No compositing here, but a lot of preliminary drawings were done, especially of the aliens. I really wanted to show some of these rough sketches, but I think I've ditched them. I normally keep almost everything, and I rarely sell my work.

Over time I came to rely on Photoshop as the place where I would bring all my pictorial elements together. A word to the wise for novices: do not color your cartoons etc. on the same layer as your Black & White (Line) Art.

Right - final inks and colors for **0007-Booty Call**. I still love these early cartoon-style ones, but I am a very slow inker, so none are planned in this style for the immediate future, even though I love this style.

Below - final inks and colors for **0004-Chat Up Line**. To see the large version of this picture, look up *Girl Crazy - The Art of Michal Dutkiewicz*, which is still available through www.sqpinc.com.

At this stage, I still felt that a picture consisting largely of just a single-figure Pin-Up was somehow 'cheating' the readers, so I tended to lay on the peripheral information and gags. Successive Editors have urged me to 'Lighten Up' my approach...

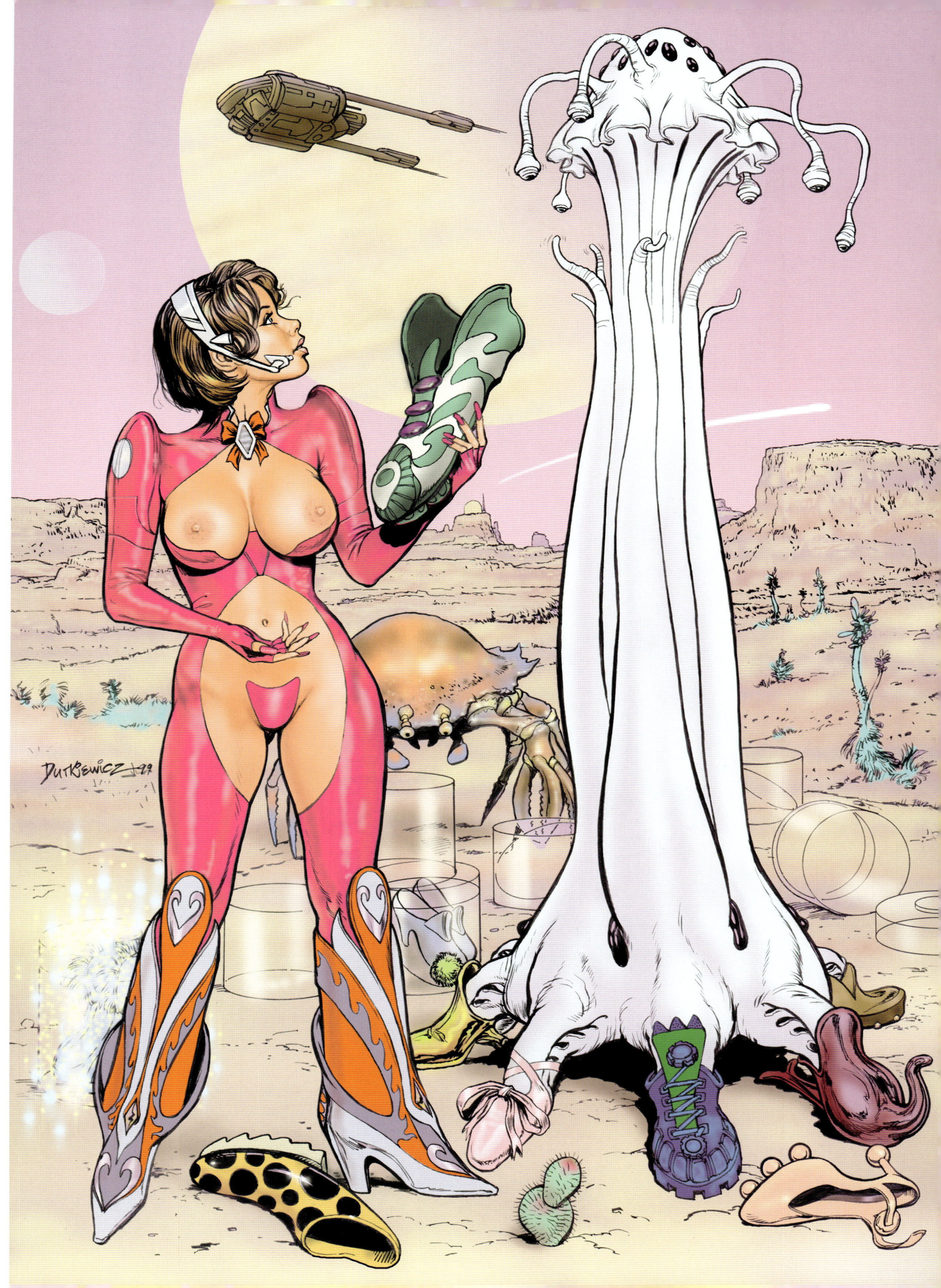

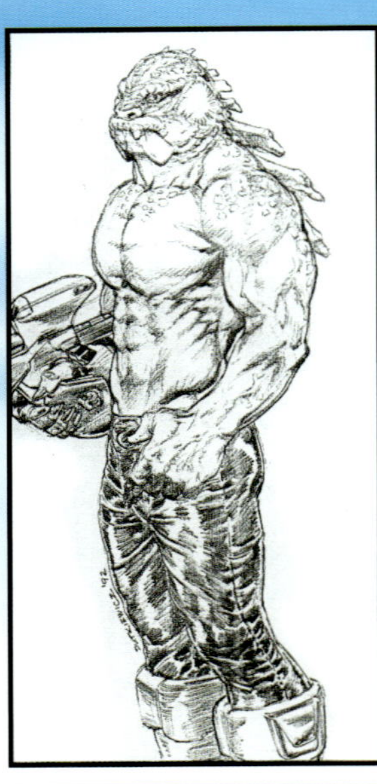

At Left and Below are two sketches completed for projects that didn't eventuate. These were both earlier attempts at creating Saurian-Human Hybrids.

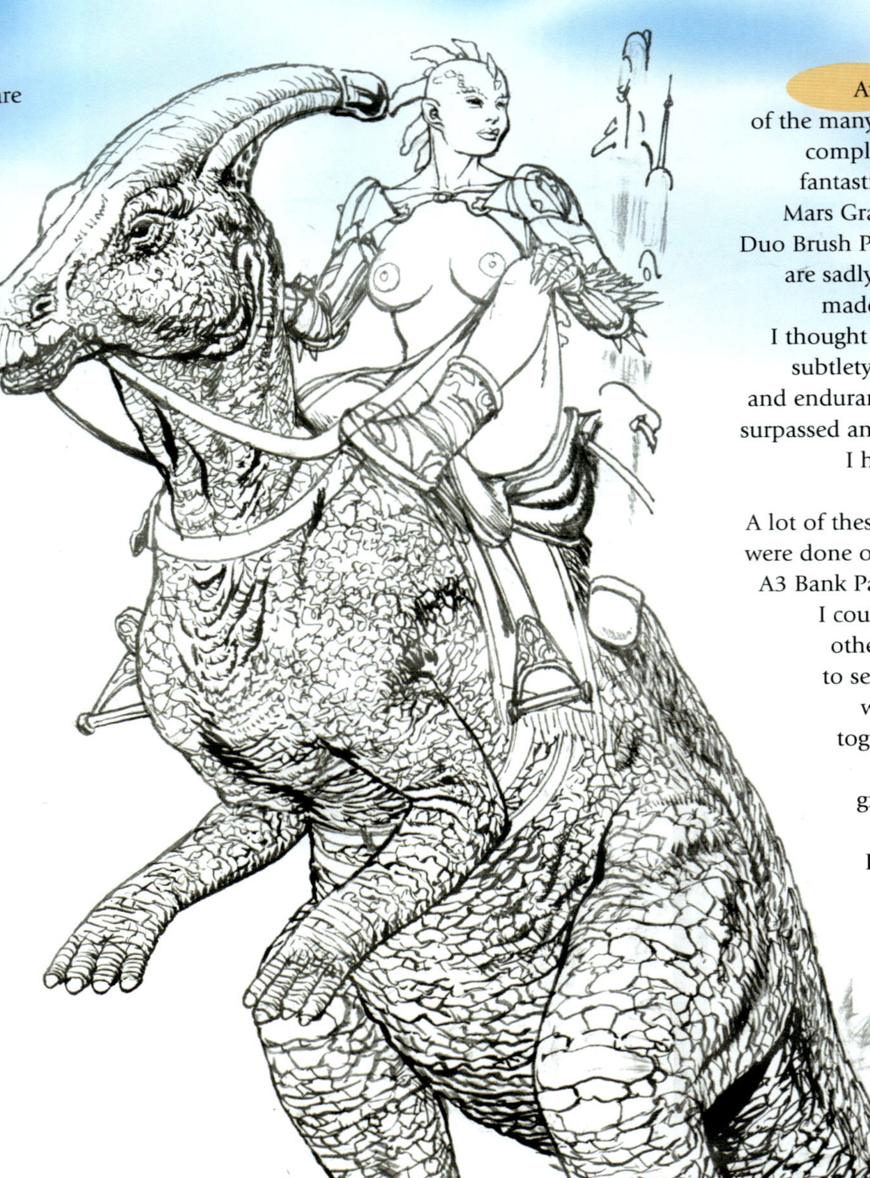

Below, and the sky at top of page, are some early attempts at digital texture-making.

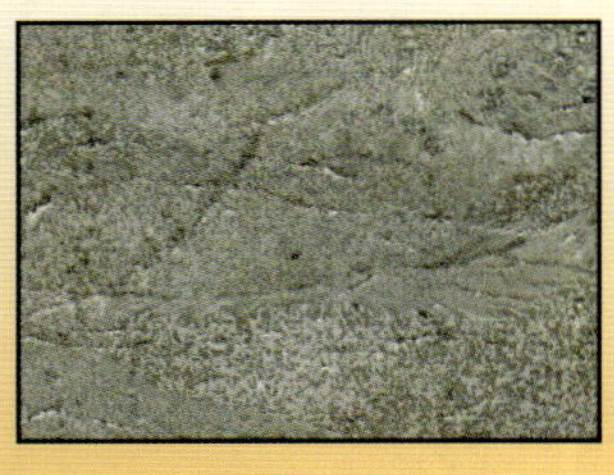

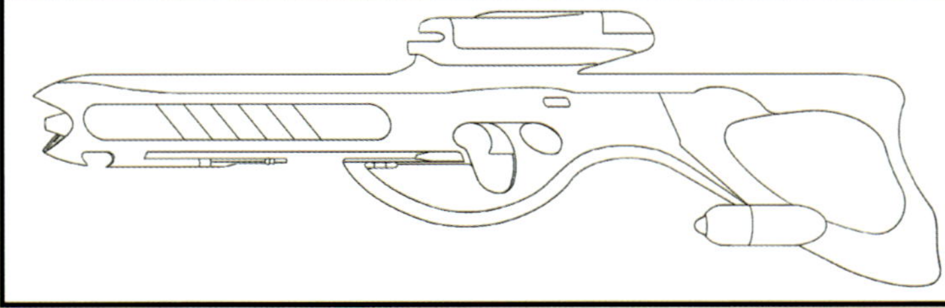

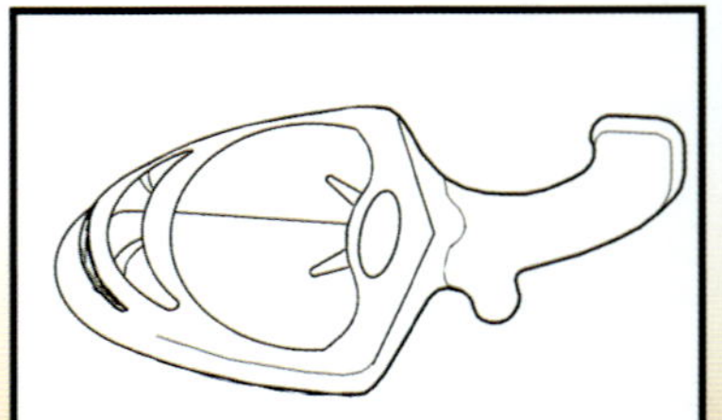

Above - a gun and a tracking device drawn in Photoshop. I wanted very clean areas for the Magic Wand Selections - used like Frisk Film in airbrushing. The materials used are not archival quality, nor were they produced with an exhibition in mind - they just needed to be scannable. Primarily, I was enthusiastically experimenting.

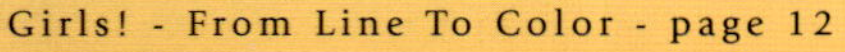

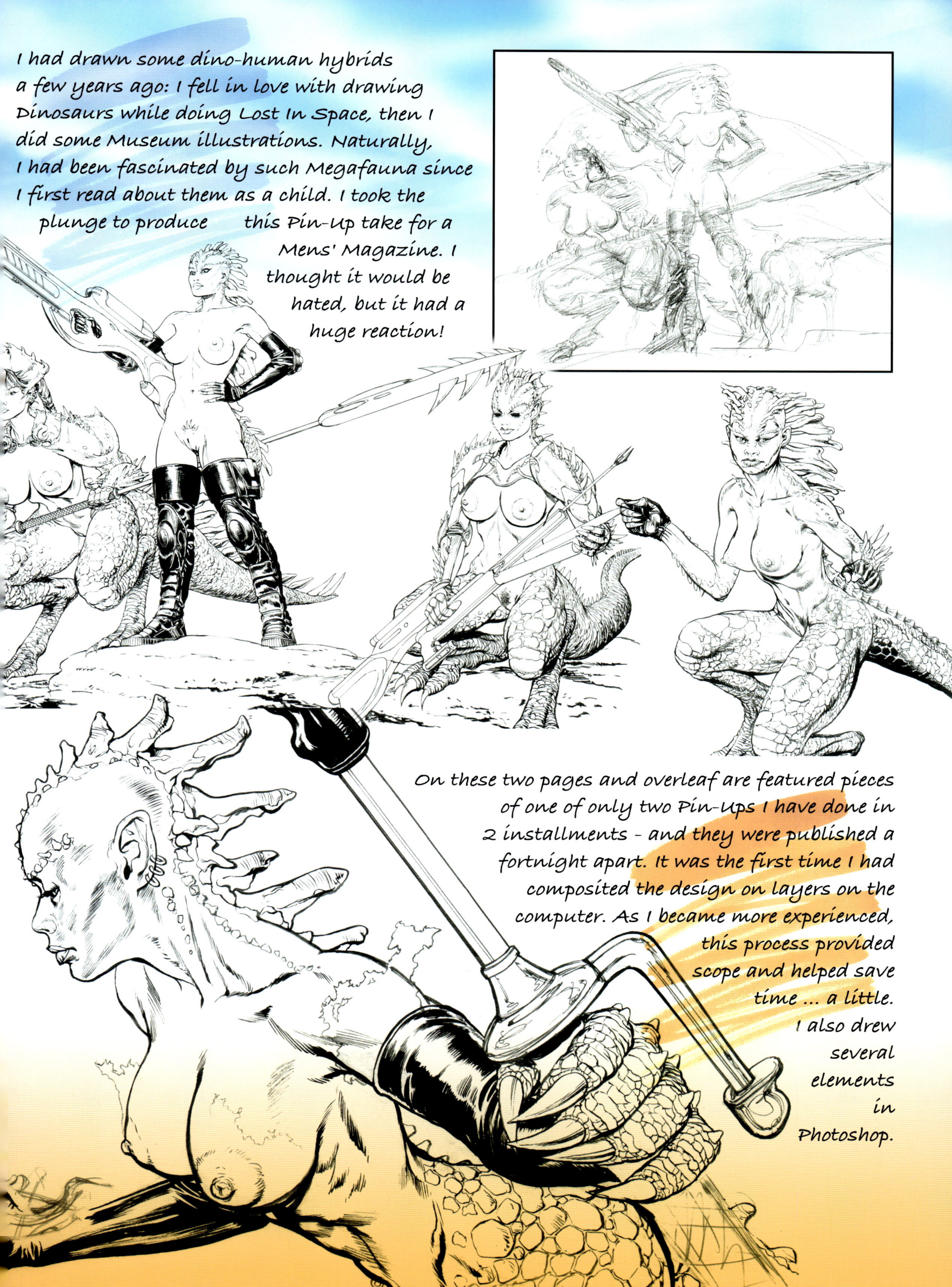

I had drawn some dino-human hybrids a few years ago: I fell in love with drawing Dinosaurs while doing Lost In Space, then I did some Museum illustrations. Naturally, I had been fascinated by such Megafauna since I first read about them as a child. I took the plunge to produce   this Pin-Up take for a Mens' Magazine. I thought it would be hated, but it had a huge reaction!

On these two pages and overleaf are featured pieces of one of only two Pin-Ups I have done in 2 installments - and they were published a fortnight apart. It was the first time I had composited the design on layers on the computer. As I became more experienced, this process provided scope and helped save time ... a little. I also drew several elements in Photoshop.

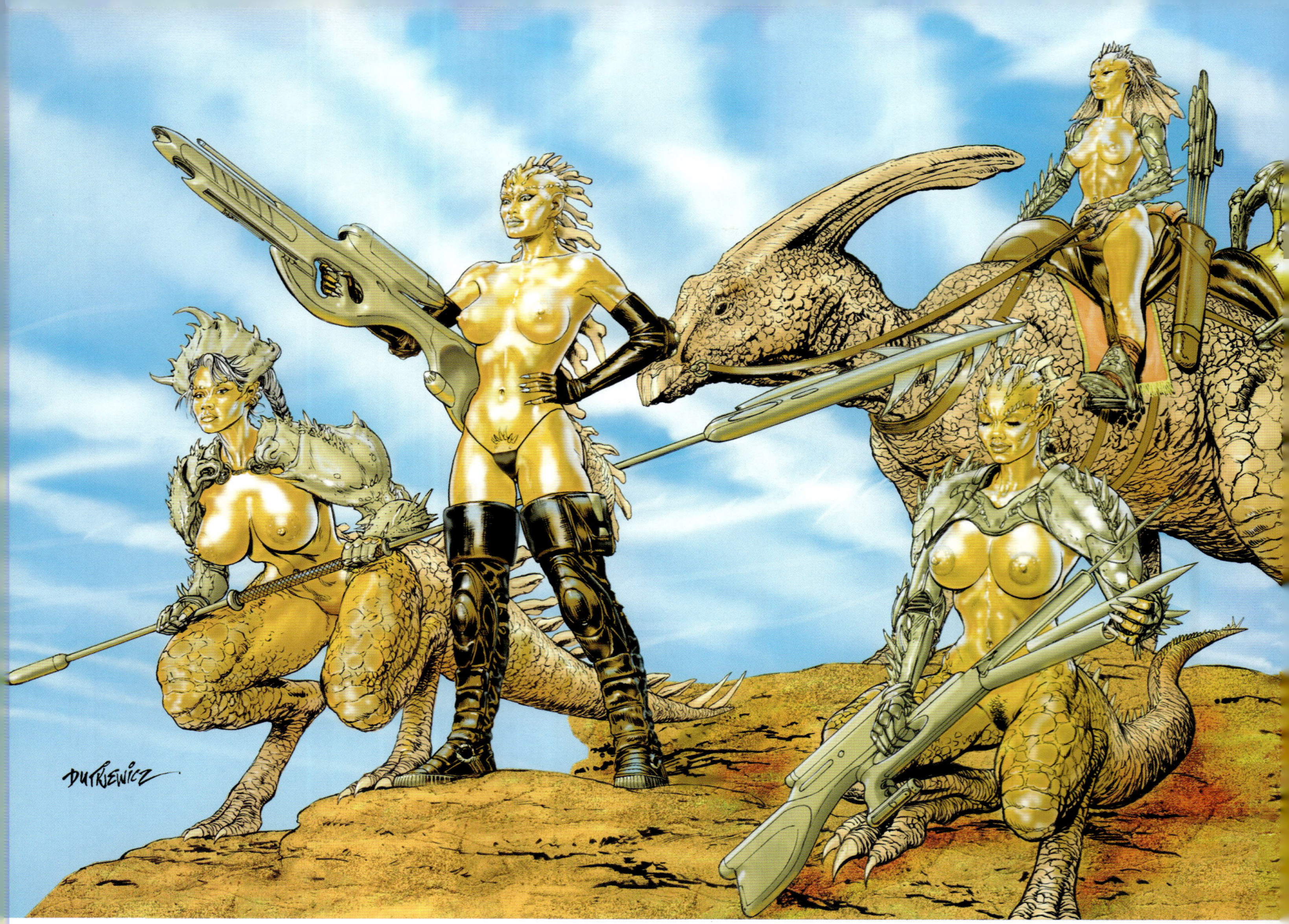

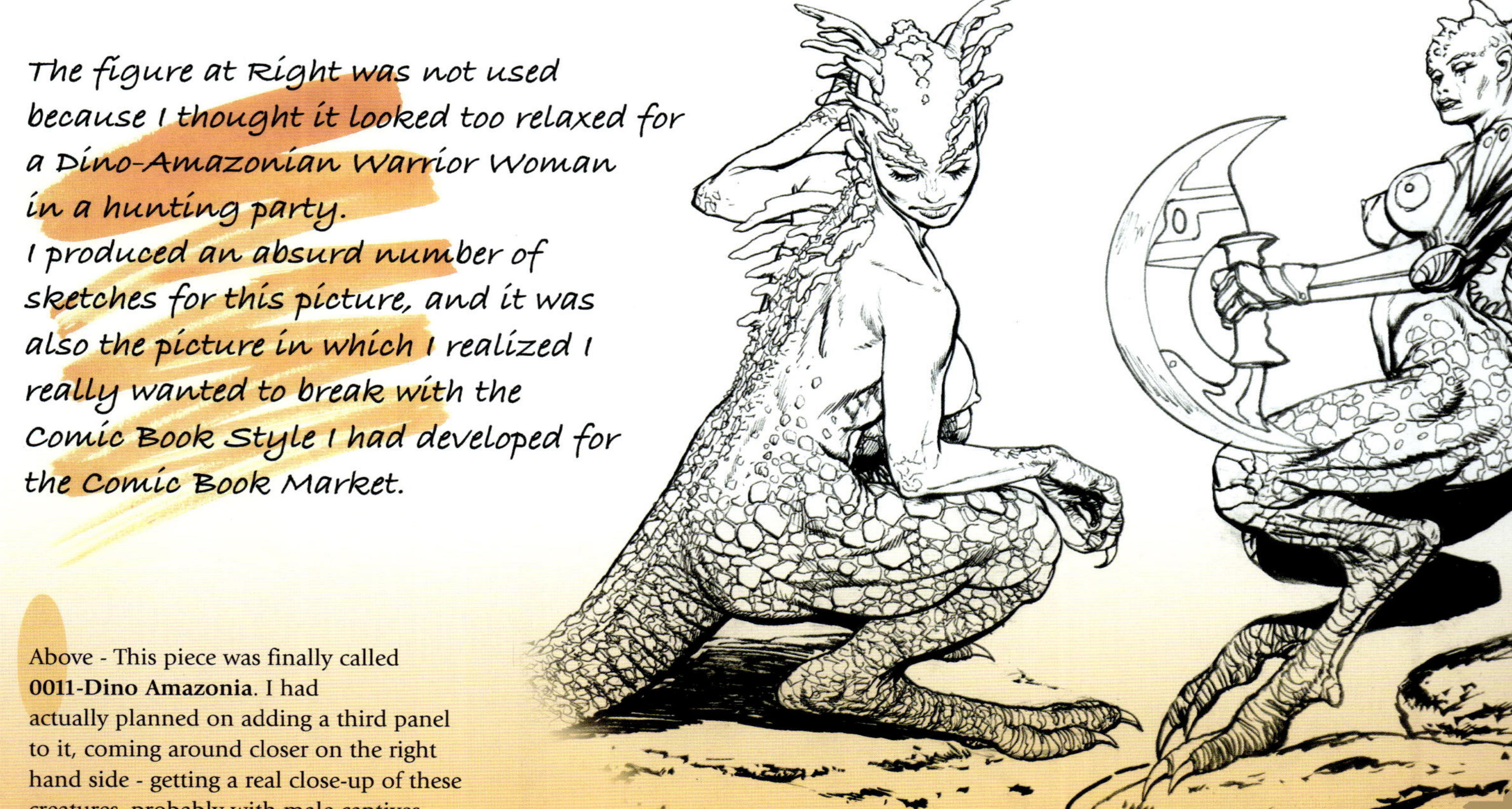

The figure at Right was not used
because I thought it looked too relaxed for
a Dino-Amazonian Warrior Woman
in a hunting party.
I produced an absurd number of
sketches for this picture, and it was
also the picture in which I realized I
really wanted to break with the
Comic Book Style I had developed for
the Comic Book Market.

Above - This piece was finally called
0011-Dino Amazonia. I had
actually planned on adding a third panel
to it, coming around closer on the right
hand side - getting a real close-up of these
creatures, probably with male captives.

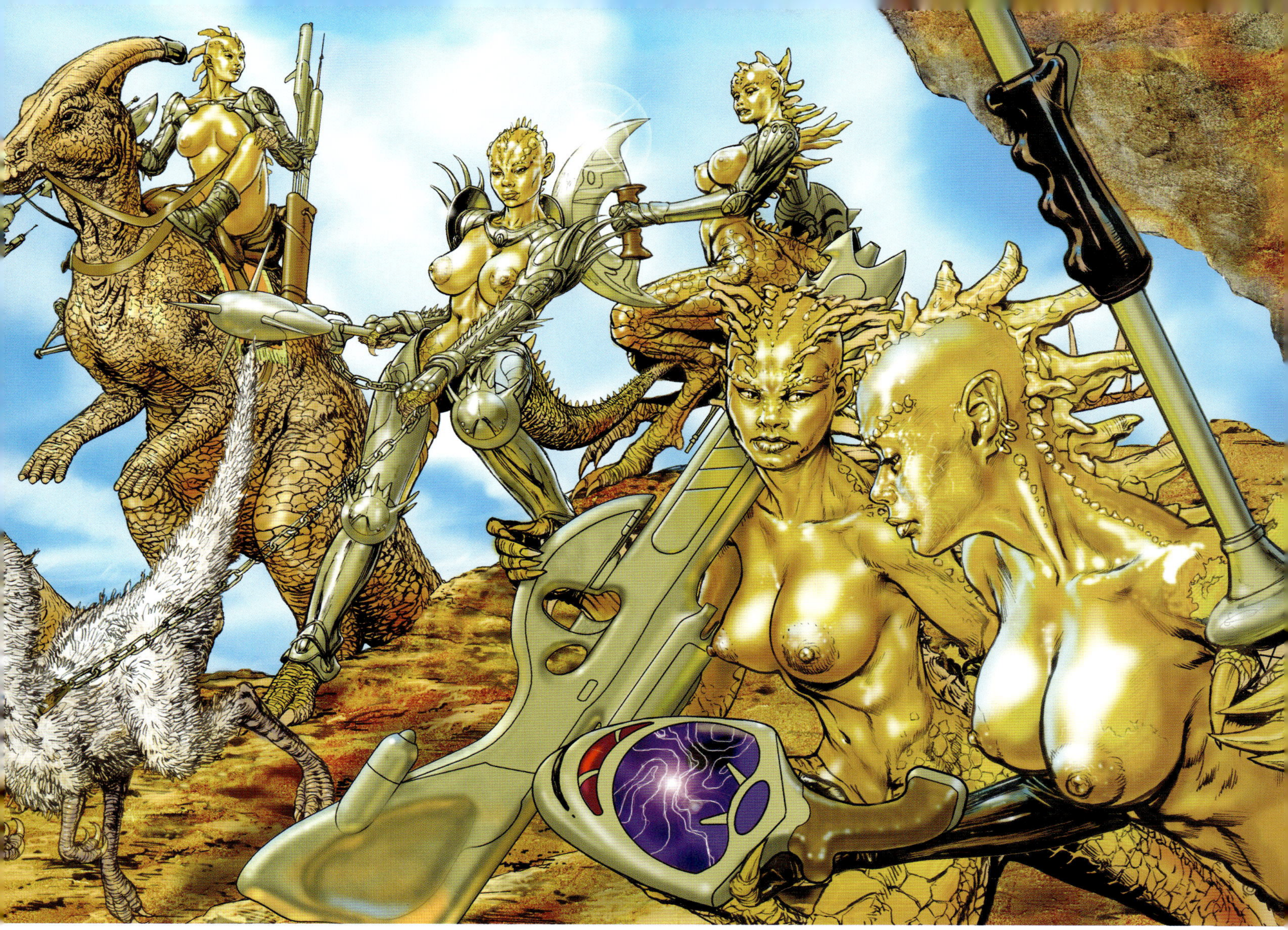

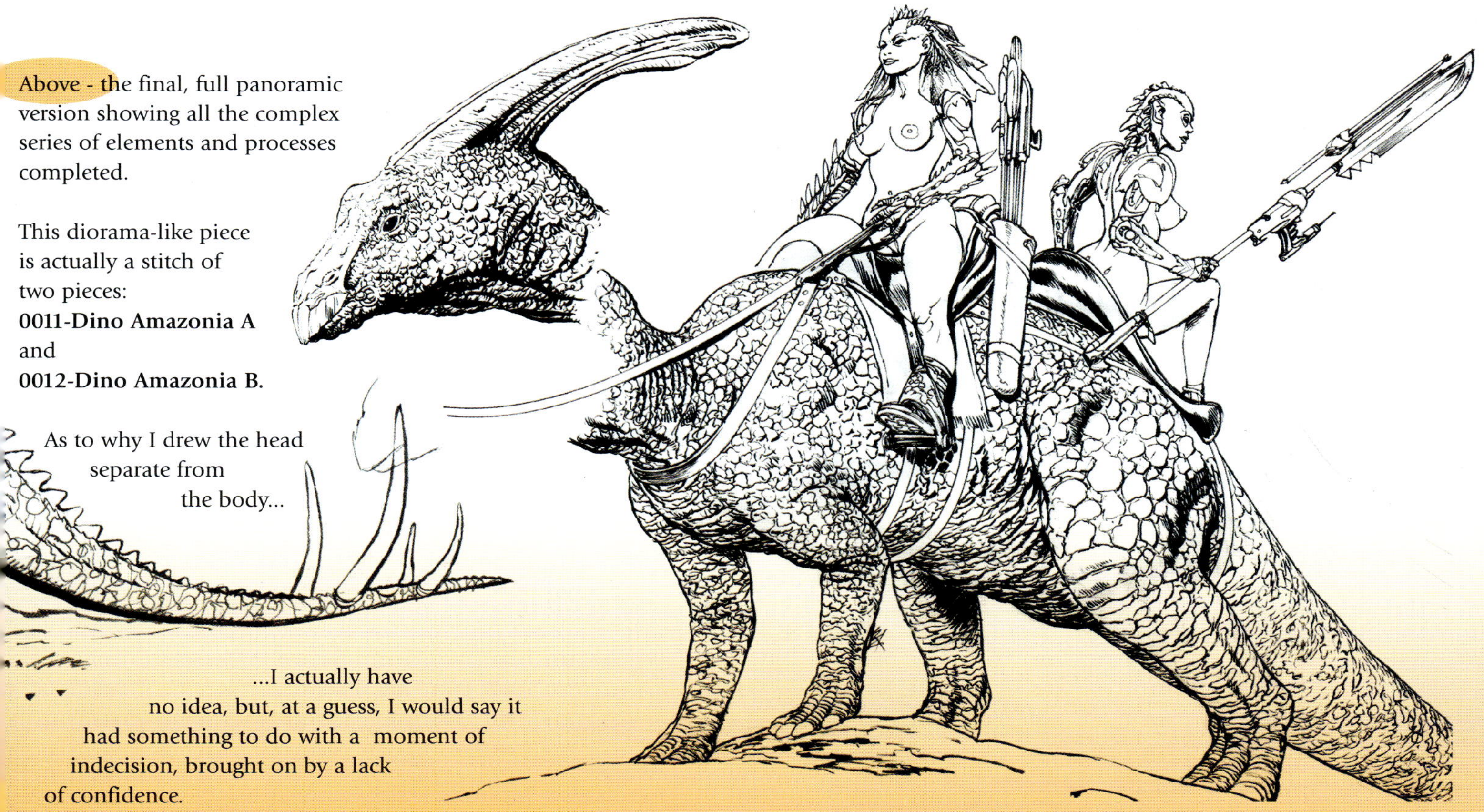

Above - the final, full panoramic
version showing all the complex
series of elements and processes
completed.

This diorama-like piece
is actually a stitch of
two pieces:
0011-Dino Amazonia A
and
0012-Dino Amazonia B.

As to why I drew the head
separate from
the body...

...I actually have
no idea, but, at a guess, I would say it
had something to do with moment of
indecision, brought on by a lack
of confidence.

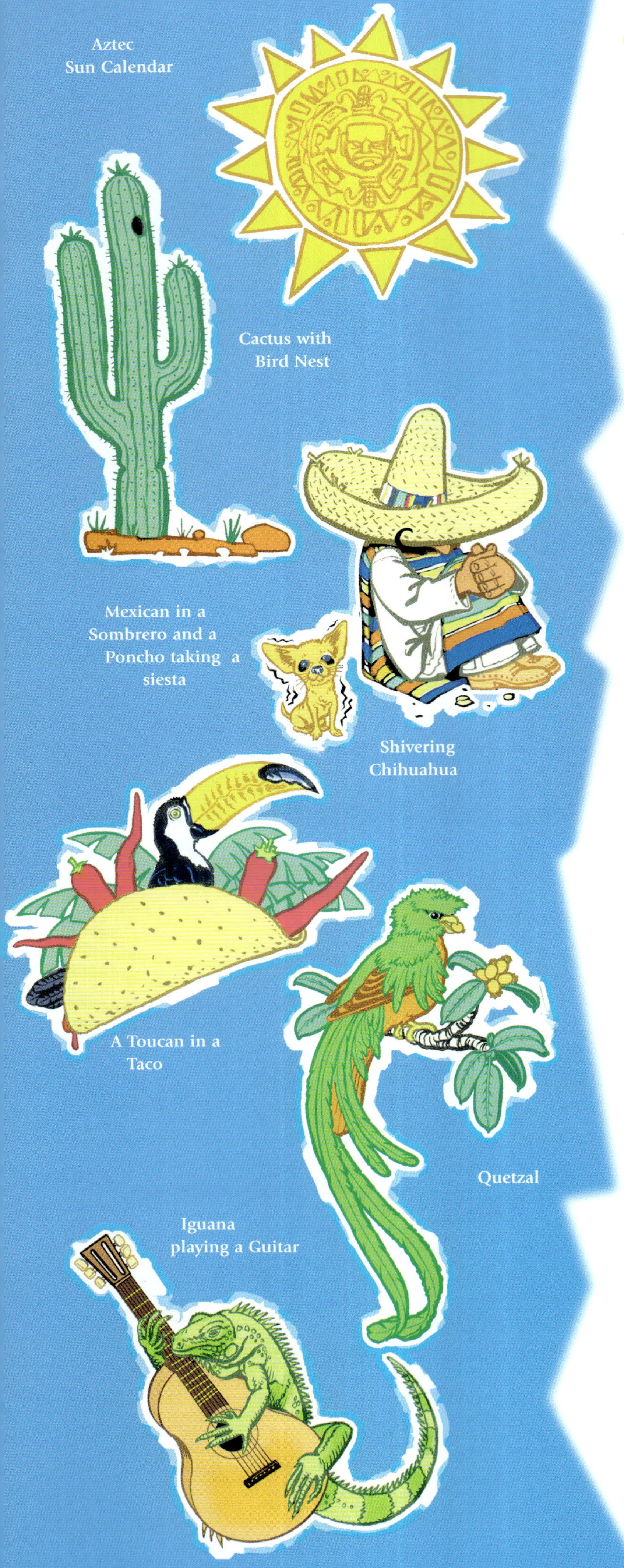

Aztec
Sun Calendar

Cactus with
Bird Nest

Mexican in a
Sombrero and a
Poncho taking a
siesta

Shivering
Chihuahua

A Toucan in a
Taco

Quetzal

Iguana
playing a Guitar

0013-Latino Lunatico - Once again I called on my favorite model, and I think this is the most number of poses derived from a single session that I have used in a single picture. I would call Guinness, but I'm a Coopers' Man - Hurrr!!

I applied color to the little decal cartoons using Screen Blending Mode on a Layer over the ink lines. I think you get more control by ticking the Group With Previous option on a new Screen Layer.

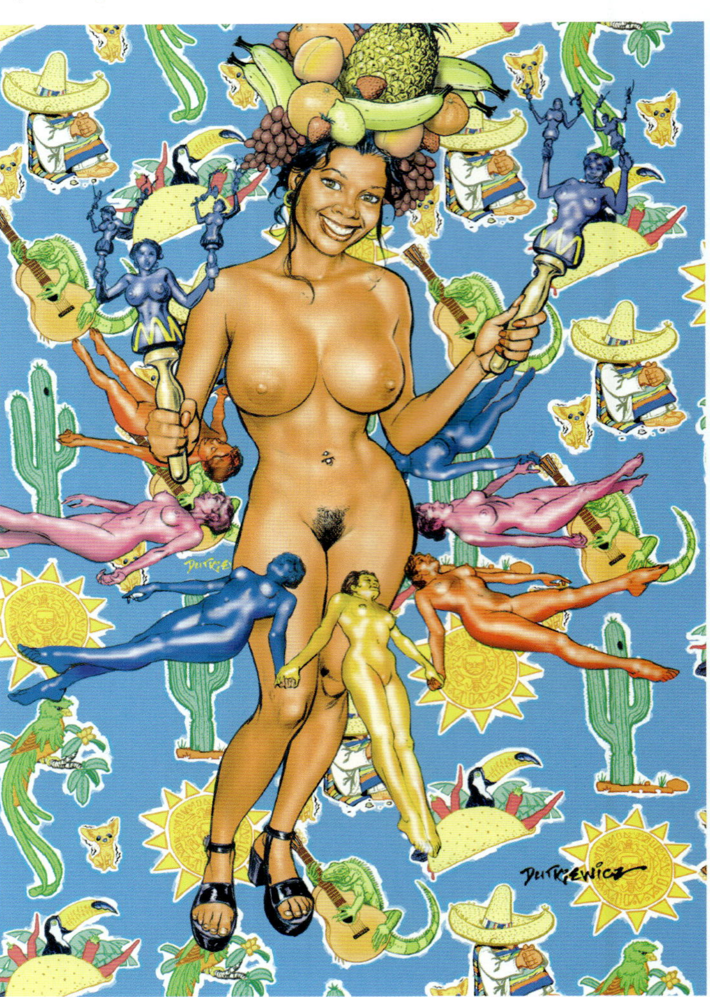

Right - 0014-Space Babe Comix Fans - Long before I was working professionally as a Comic Book Illustrator, I had fallen under the spell of Wally Wood, Frank Frazetta and Al Williamson. The black and white picture was done as a favor for someone, and I dusted it off years later, my favorite model in tow, who was fortunately living in my hometown at the time, and carefully posed her to make maximum use of the good stuff in the old version of the picture.

I don't know any kids today who have quite the same fascination with Space as those who watched the Moon Landing.

Once, as a child, I won an art competition with a picture, 30 inches by 40 inches, of an Astronaut in a flaming capsule...

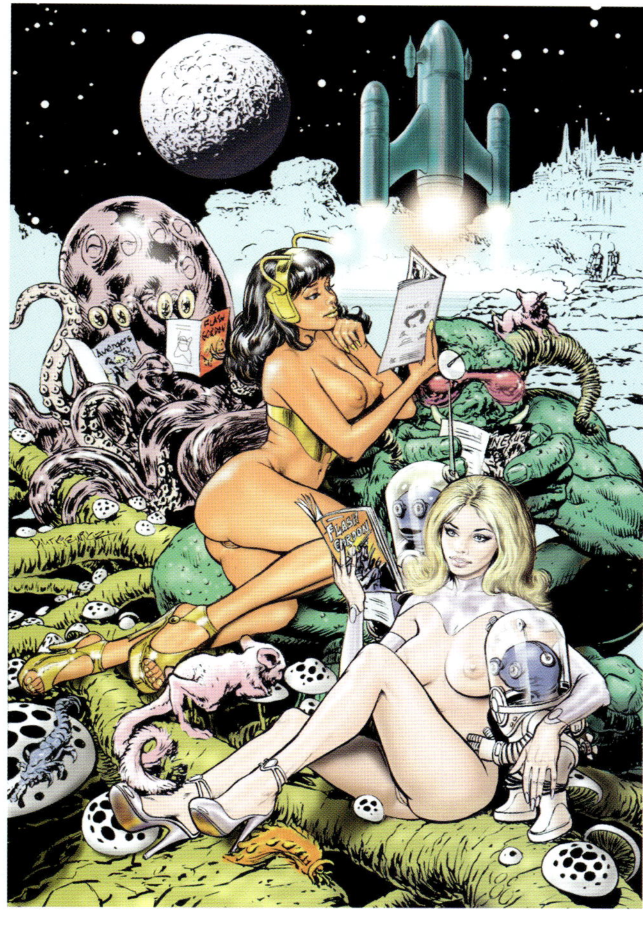

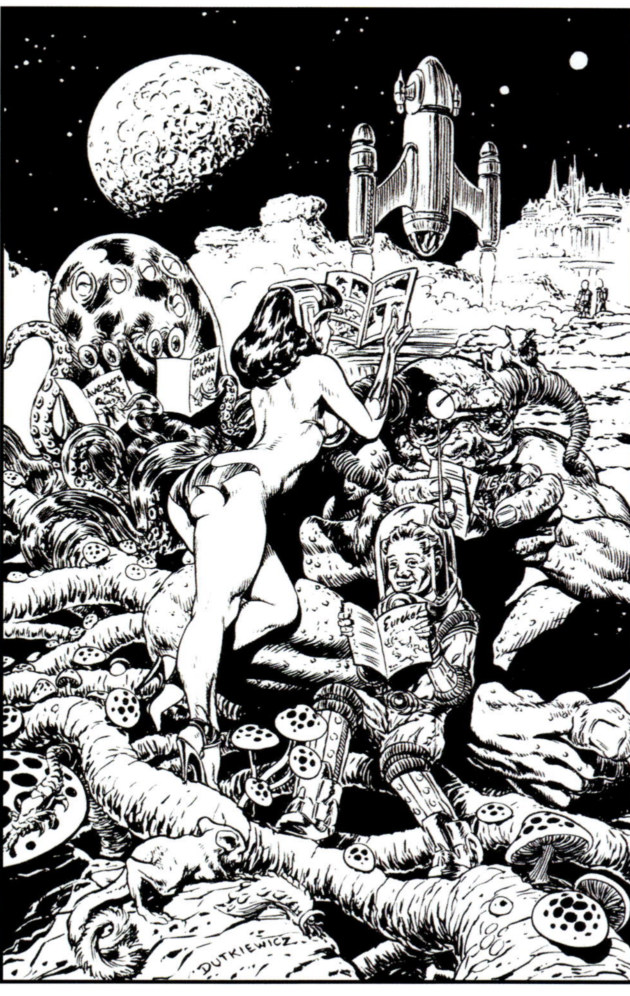

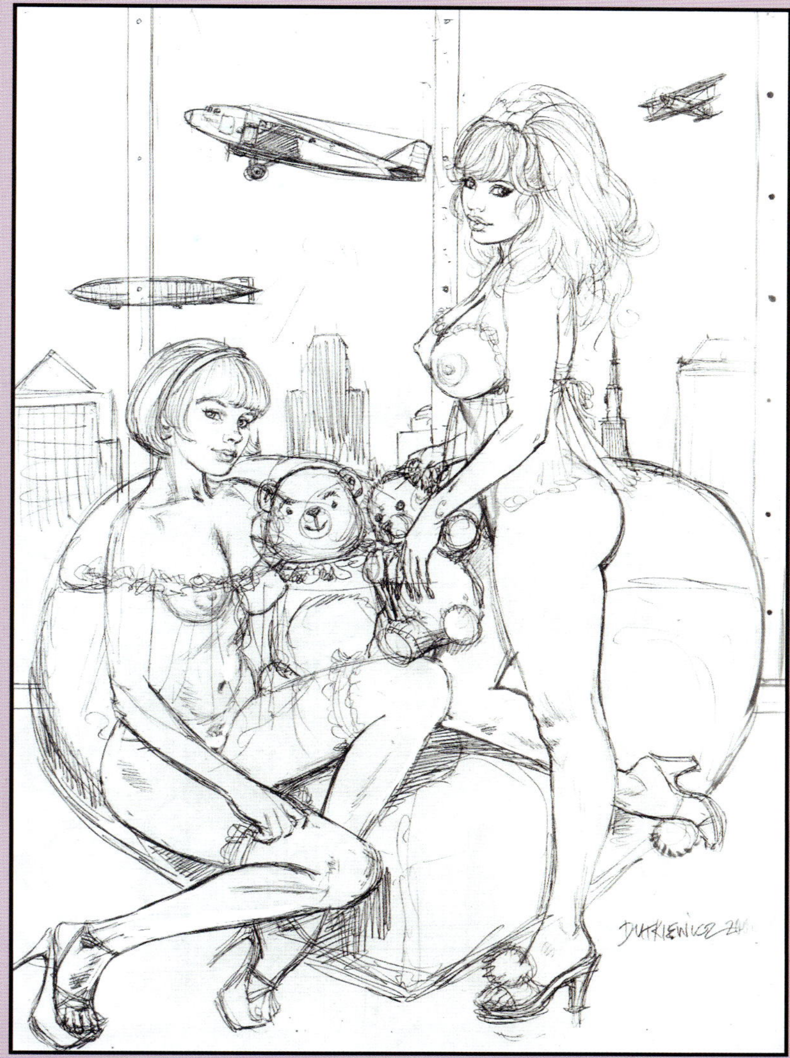

0010-Fluffy Airheads - In my book, *Girl Crazy, The Art of Michal Dutkiewicz*, I have already talked a bit about the intended significance of my Pin-Ups. But this was one time when what I wanted to do was influenced by an Editor. I had submitted the sketch above to him at the pencil stage because I was concerned that it might bug the censors. He warned me that the Teddy Bears could be a problem, so I completely rethought the picture. And I am very, very happy I did - it's so CREEPY!!!

It also made me think harder about what I wanted to say. There are some things about this picture I really would rather people work out for themselves - or just enjoy.

The alternative title was: **0010-Fools' Paradise.**

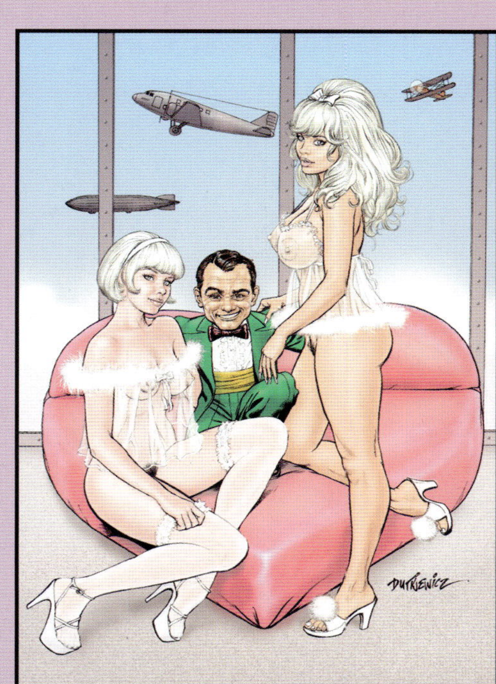

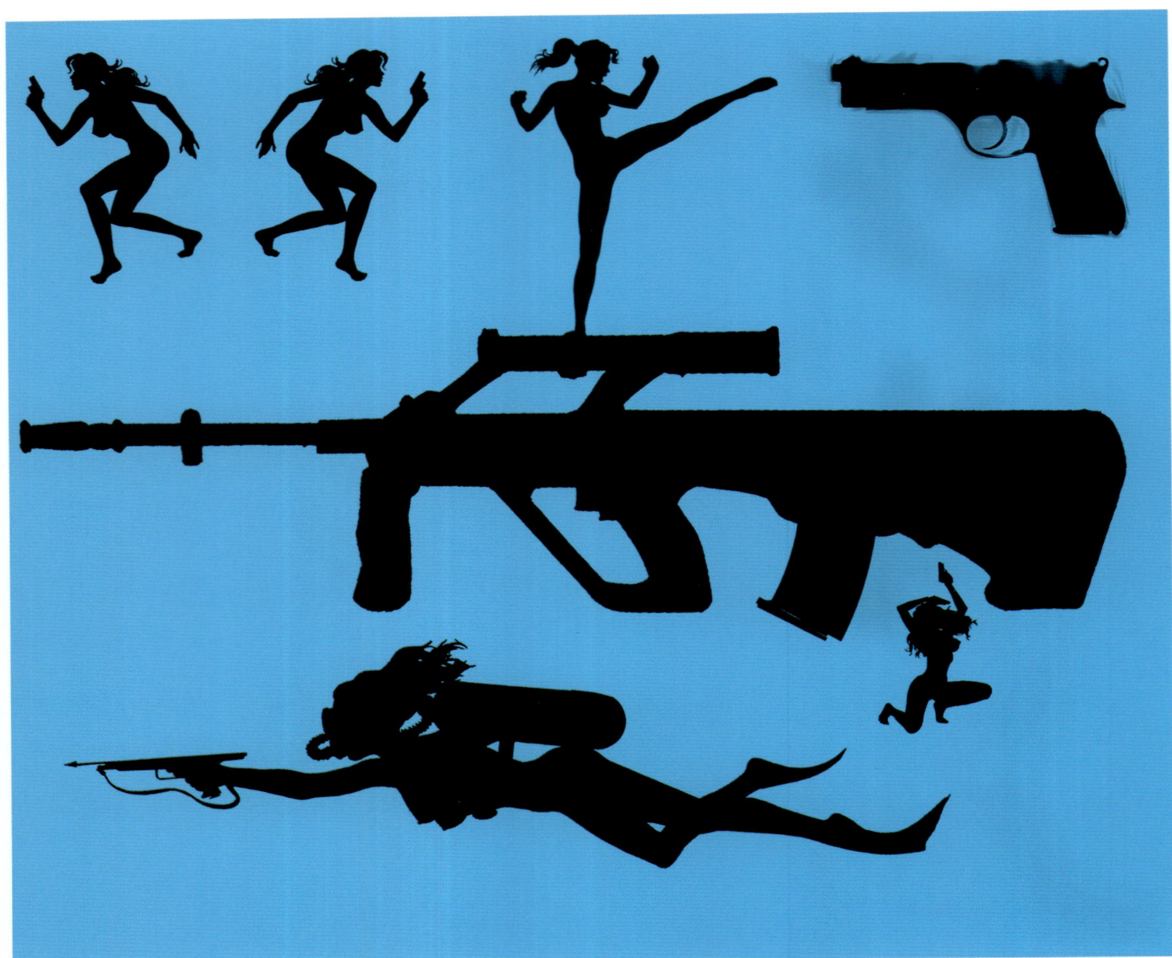

Left - the
silhouettes of
Maurice Binder,
and countless 60s'
TV shows were
a key atmosphere
point for
0016-Action Minxes.

These were all
done as separate
pieces and then
composited in
Photoshop.

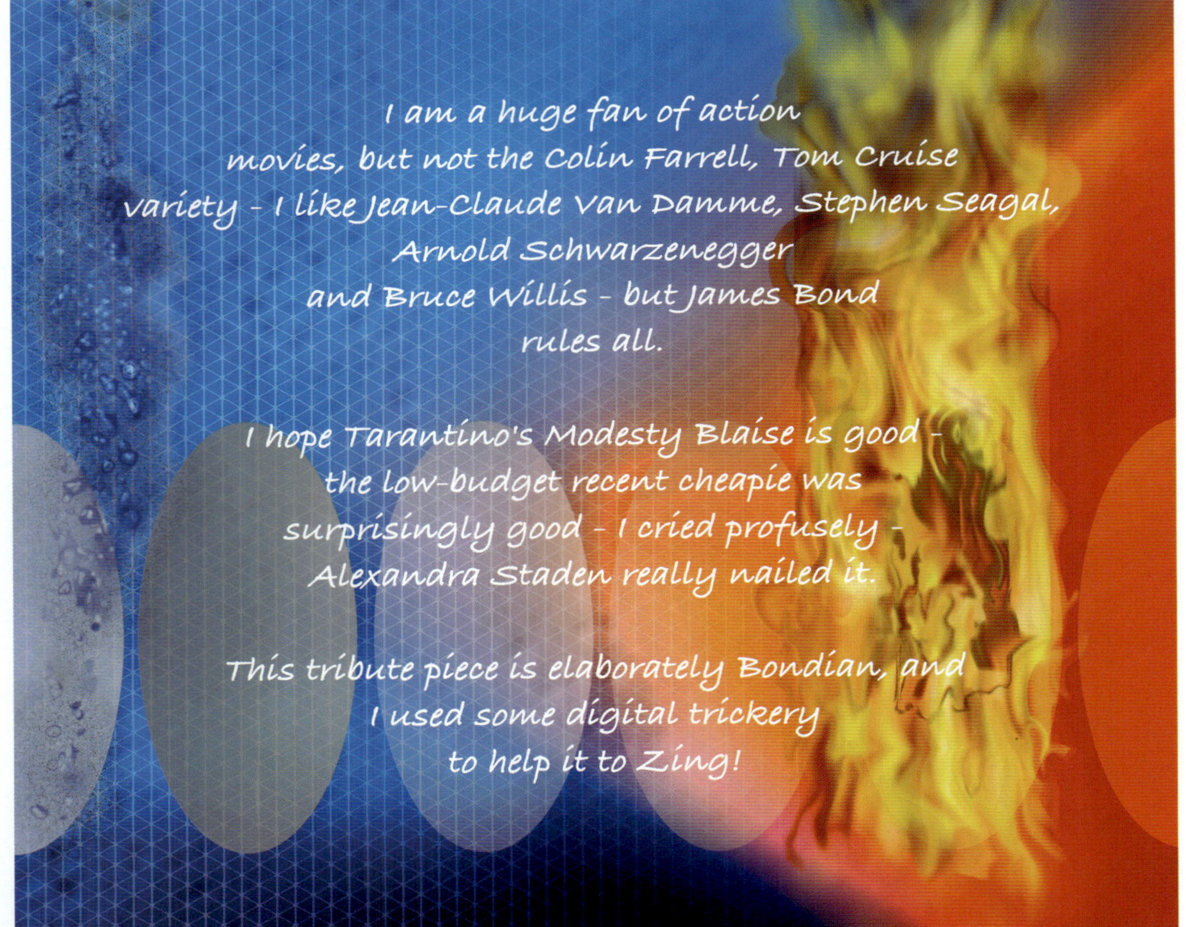

I am a huge fan of action
movies, but not the Colin Farrell, Tom Cruise
variety - I like Jean-Claude Van Damme, Stephen Seagal,
Arnold Schwarzenegger
and Bruce Willis - but James Bond
rules all.

I hope Tarantino's Modesty Blaise is good -
the low-budget recent cheapie was
surprisingly good - I cried profusely -
Alexandra Staden really nailed it.

This tribute piece is elaborately Bondian, and
I used some digital trickery
to help it to Zing!

Left - Once again,
in the color
background there
were several
must-have
thematic elements.

This was one of
the first times I
seriously
exploited the possible,
complex and different
combinations that
wowed me with
the potential of the
Layers Blending
Modes Menu in
Photoshop.

Right - I really hated
much of the extreme,
cool Image Comics-
style body language of
the Action girls in 90s'
comics. I thought
Natural-Born Killers
better represented
the 90s.

In my figures and faces I
wanted to evoke the
more personality-driven
characters from
classier 'action vehicles'.

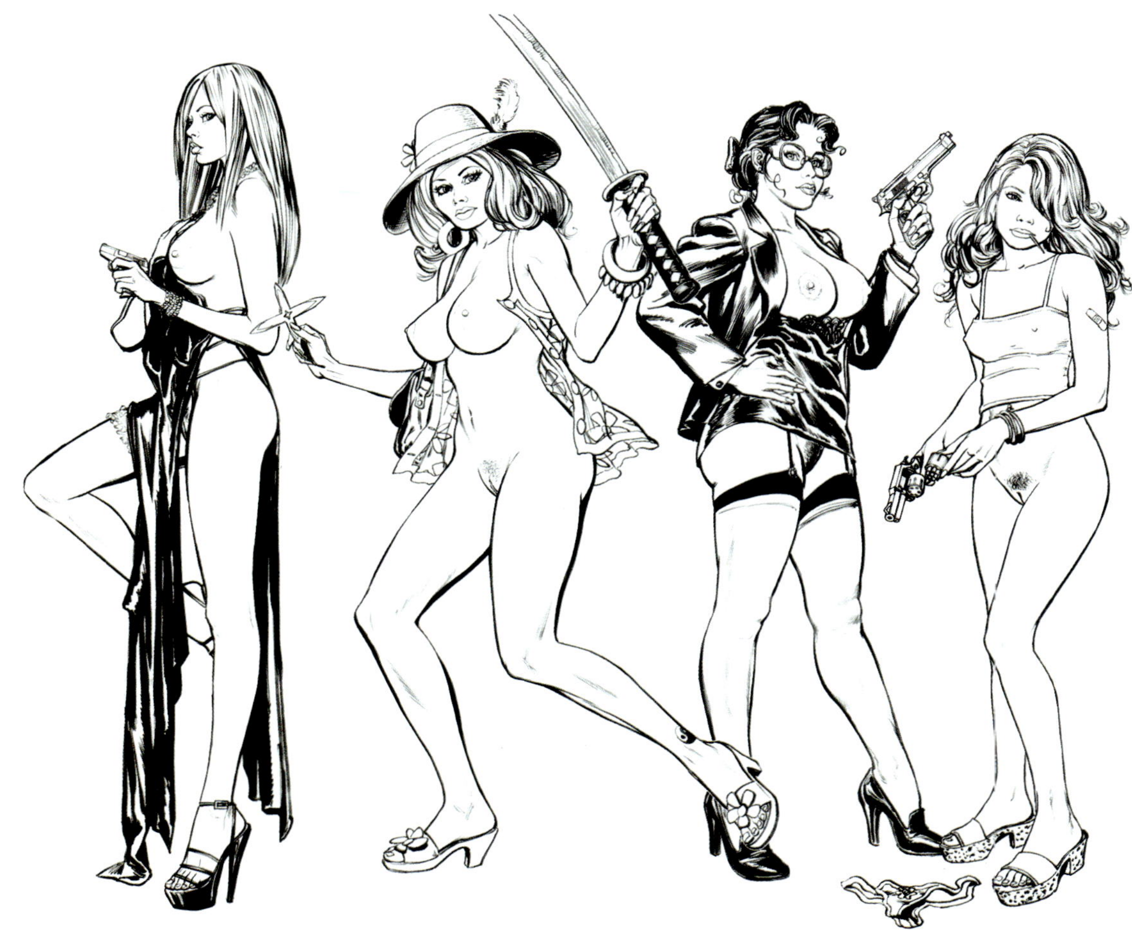

Right - Finally,
when it was all
composited, I found
myself really wishing
my editors would
allow me to do a
more realistic, less
comic-book style.
Little did I know that
the change I was
wrestling with,
thinking I was
committing an act
of heresy, was
exactly what they
wanted...

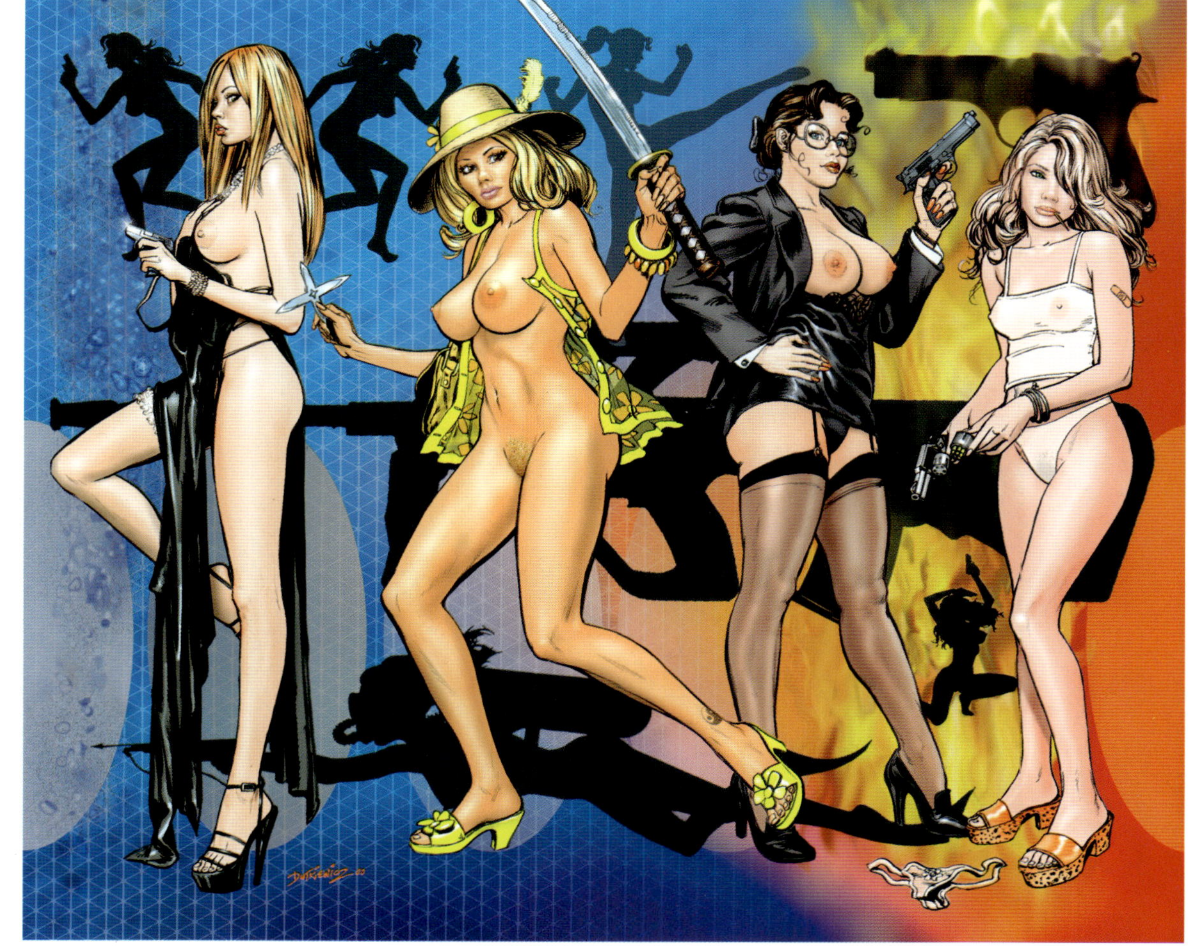

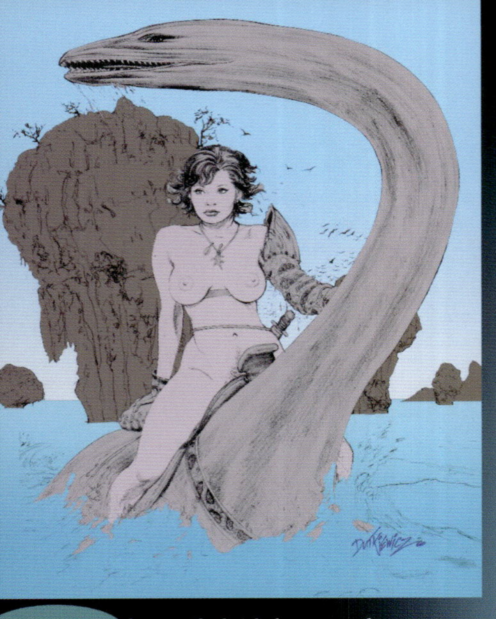

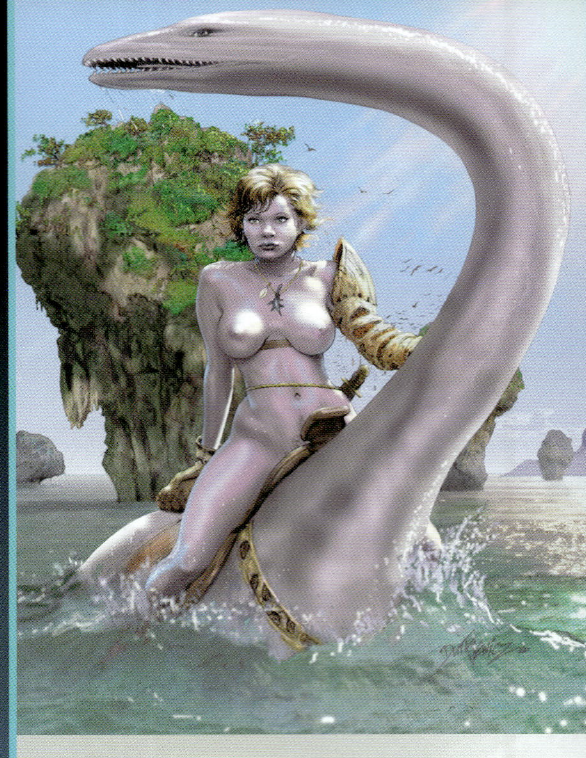

Above - Final pencils laid down and
Selections made for masking areas to paint.

Below - the rough sketch for **0044-Behemoth Rider 01.**
This was a relatively complete sketch that contained most of the
elements for the finished piece, although not the Phuket Sound-like
background. The idea is that both creatures breathe under and
above water. The plesiosauroid is supposed to be a Cetacean.

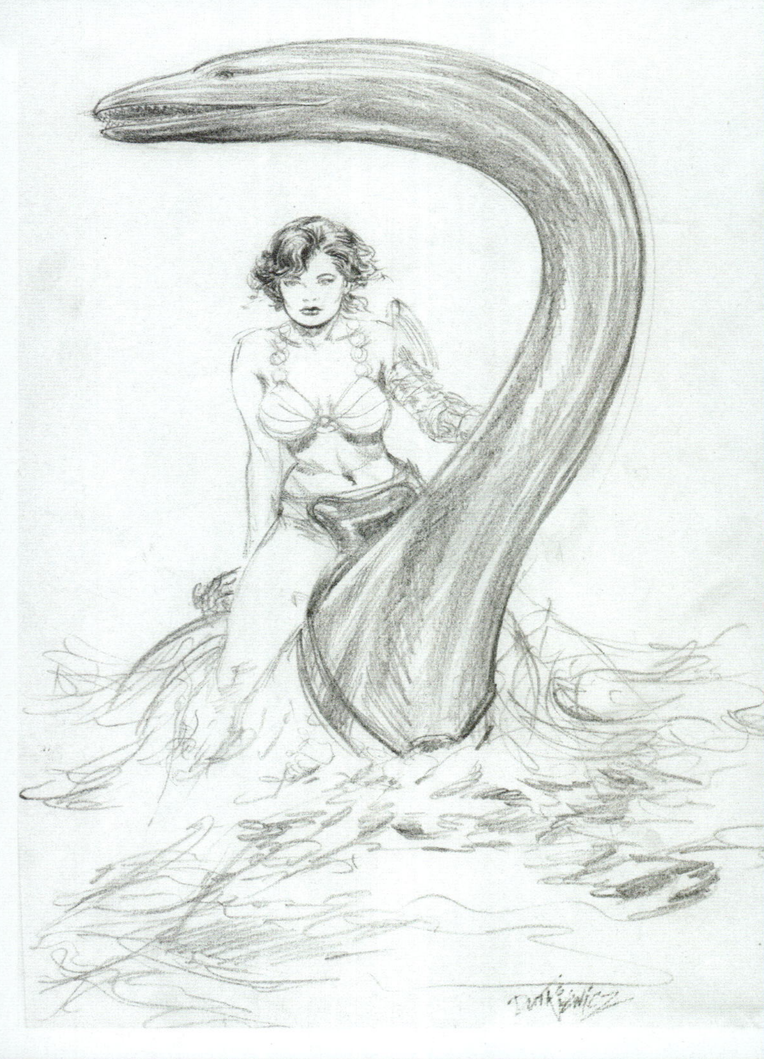

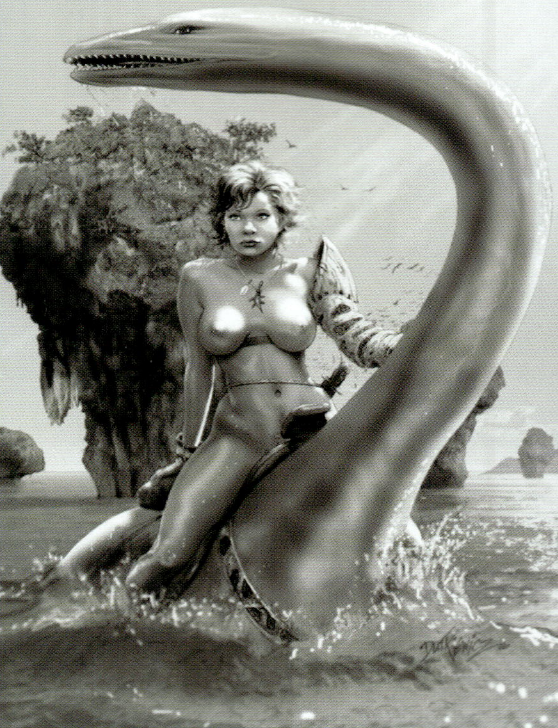

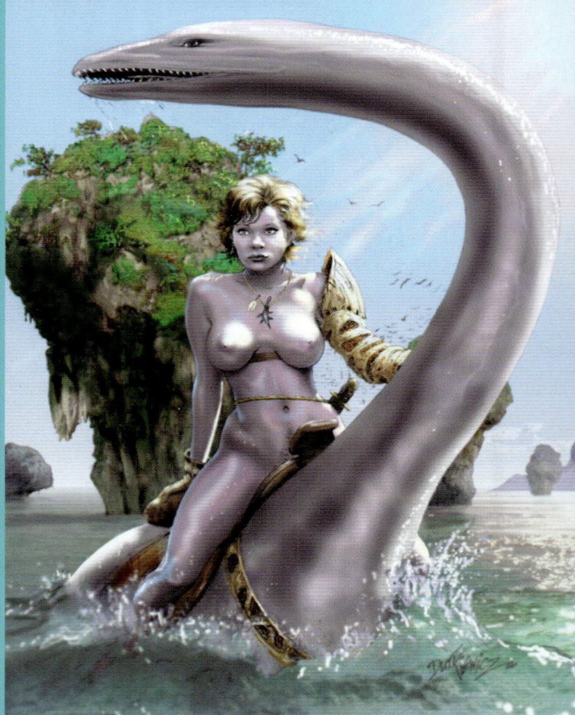

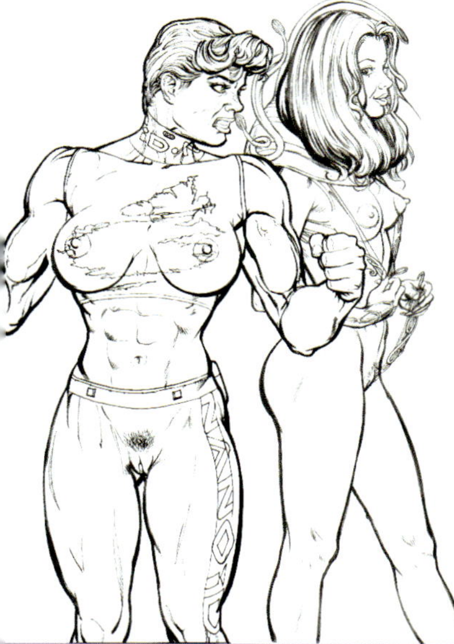

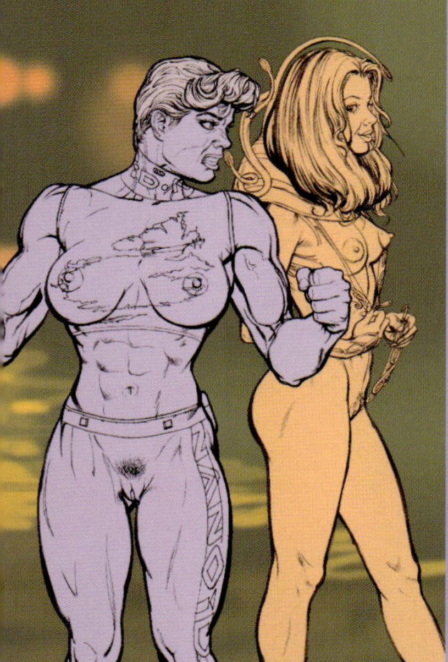

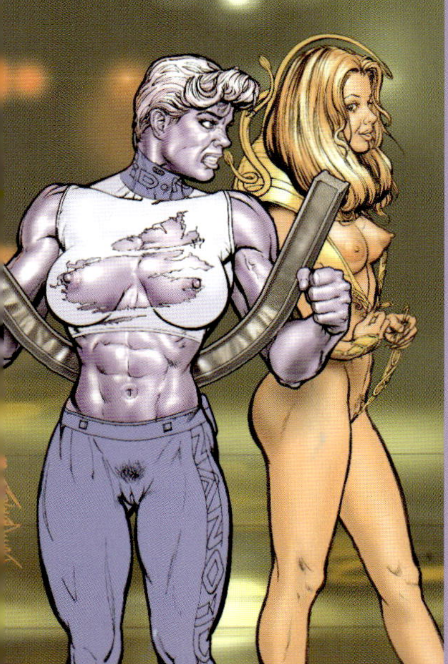

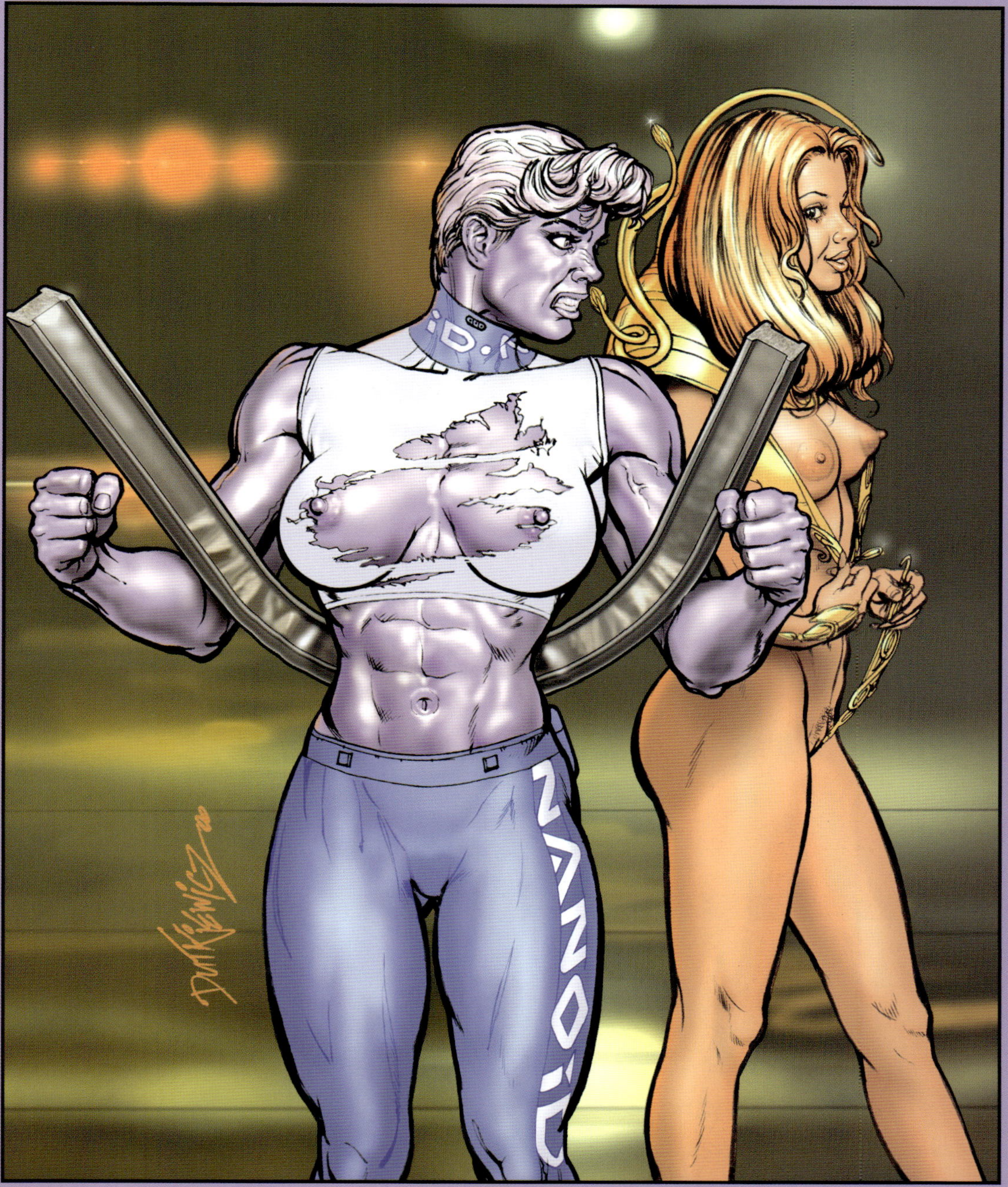

Above - Final colors for 0026-**Nanoid and Alchemyst.**
I feel some of the coloring in this one looks very rushed now. It was a very early attempt
at using Dodge and Burn tools set on combinations of Highlights, Mid Tones and Shadows.
This is about as basic a job of coloring as you could get - clean and simple.

Above - Stages from composite
through to start of final colors.
Note the background changes.

Nanoid and Alchemyst are two characters from a proposed
erotic comic strip that a friend and I have been developing.
They represent raw power and its antithesis - guile and
seduction.
I have quite a few properties that, by necessity, will remain in
the drawer until I can find time to get to them...

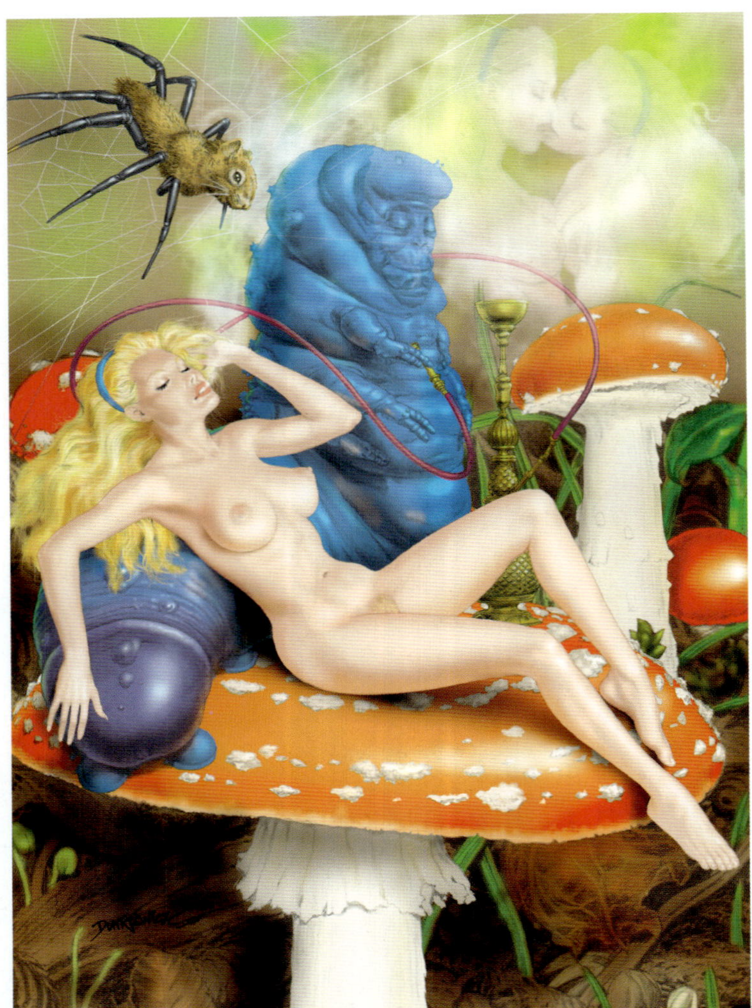

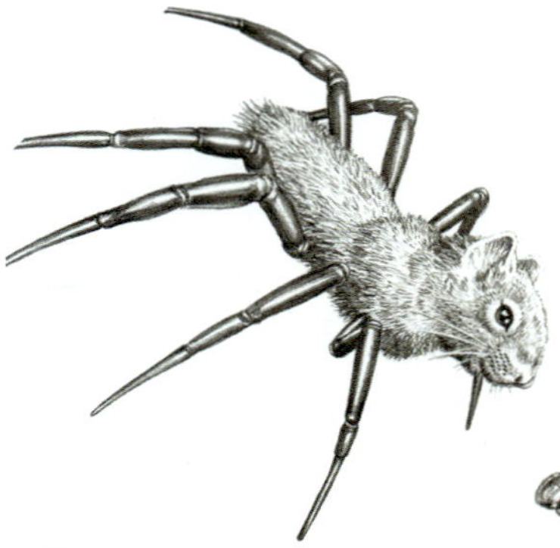

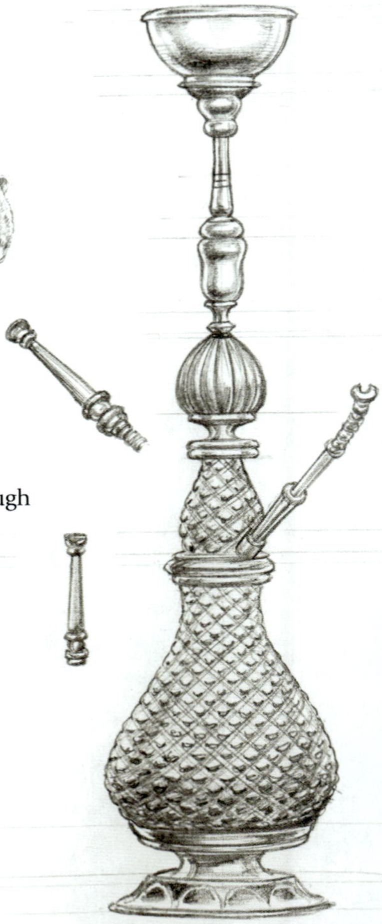

I handed this one in nervously.
I was ready to make
every apology in the book
for the abrupt change of
style and direction for this
Pin-Up.

I didn't have a chance to
say much - the ed. was
raving about it and how he
wanted me to try more
like this.

Unfortunately, this would
mean many more sleepless
nights. Seven years without
a regular sleep pattern takes
its toll. Maybe that's what
this pic is about...

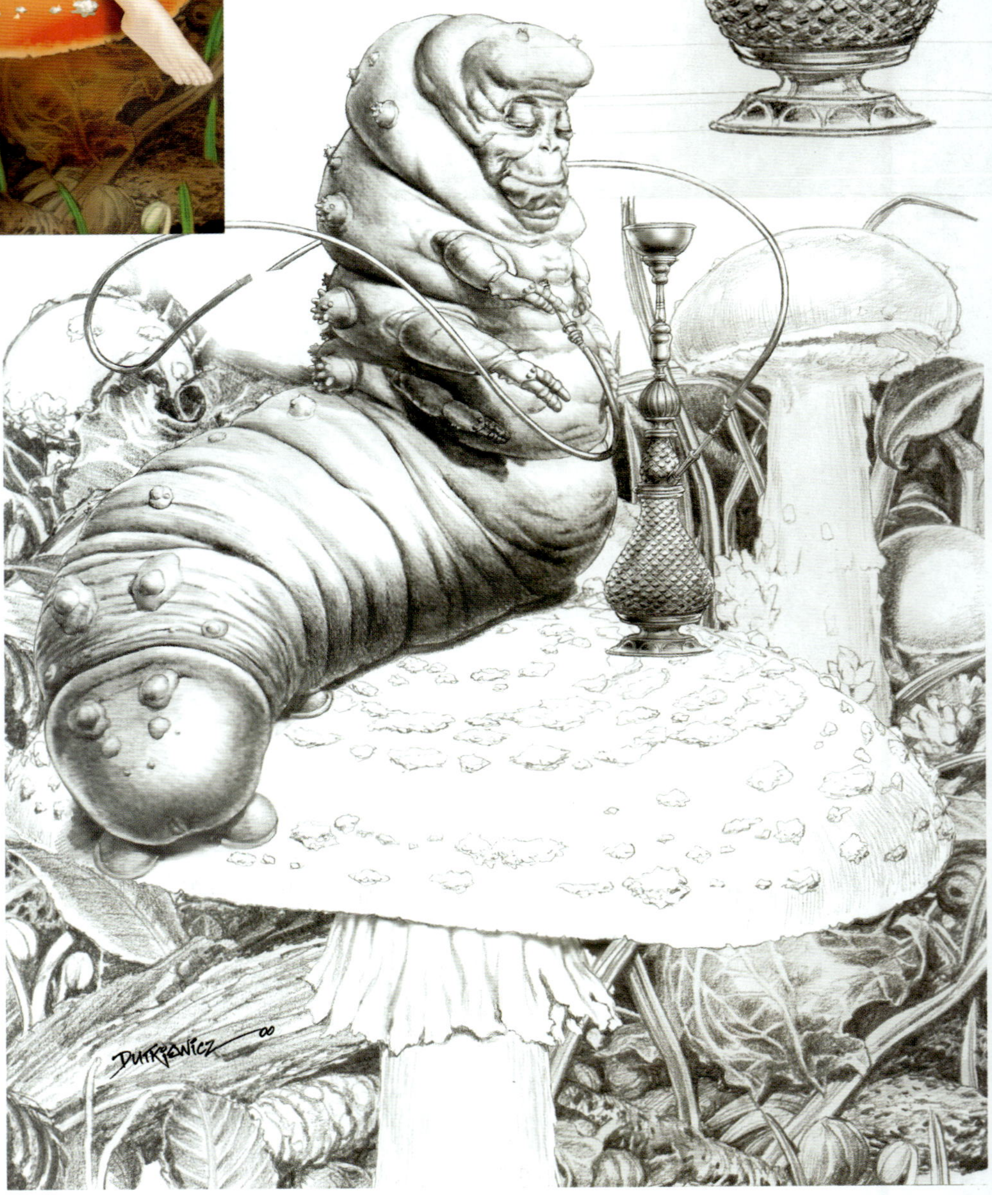

A year or so after I went full-time on pin-ups, I commenced a series of more sexually explicit pictures for a magazine called Picture Premium. The regular weekly pin-up was for the softer Picture magazine.

I completed some 30 explicit pin-ups on a monthly basis, plus a few 4-page, one-shot, erotic, full-color comics pieces. But I just got too swamped with other work, especially the film conceptualizing: illustration and a bit of writing.

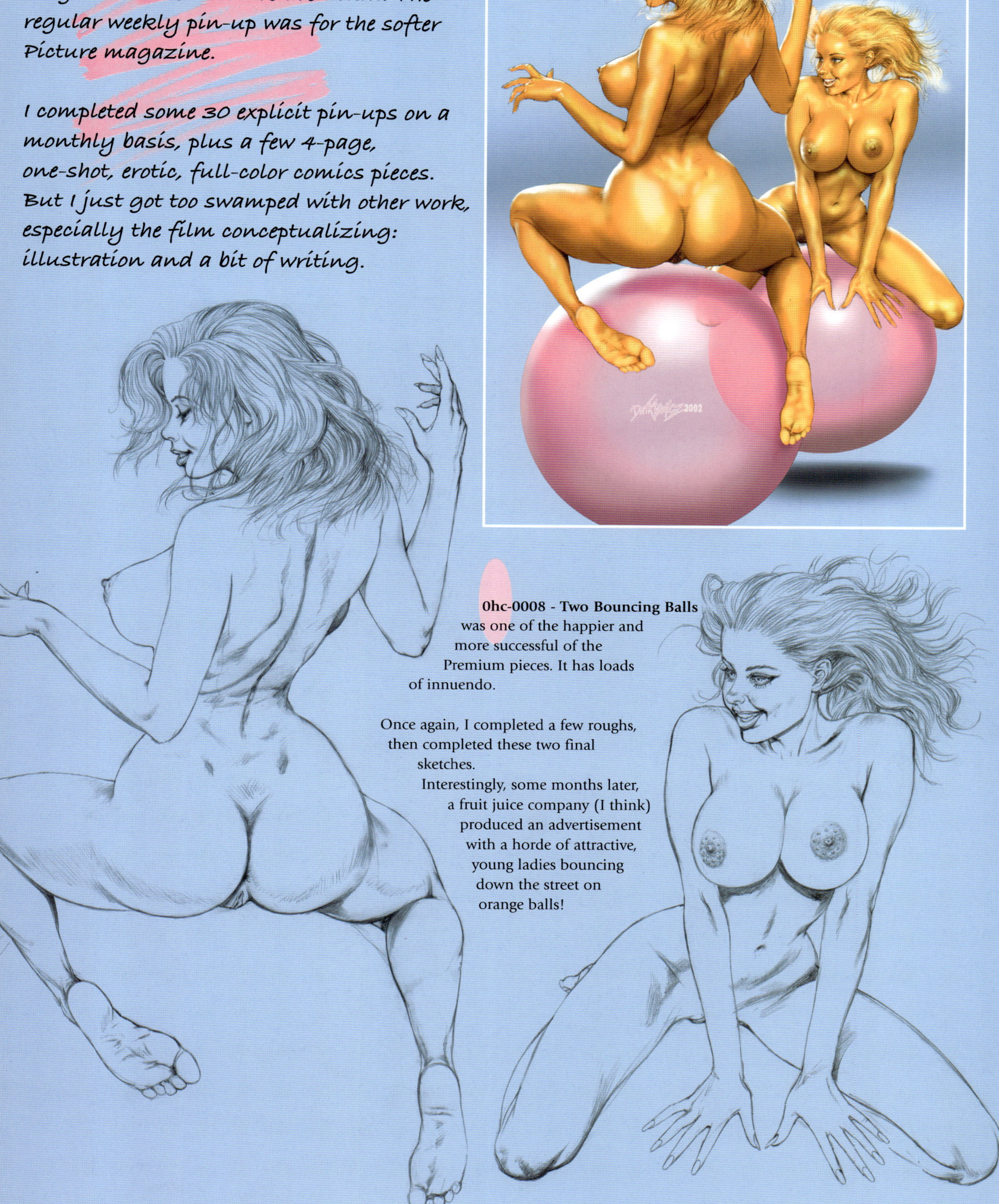

0hc-0008 - Two Bouncing Balls was one of the happier and more successful of the Premium pieces. It has loads of innuendo.

Once again, I completed a few roughs, then completed these two final sketches.
Interestingly, some months later, a fruit juice company (I think) produced an advertisement with a horde of attractive, young ladies bouncing down the street on orange balls!

This panel shows just
the unadorned, raw
pencils for this job.
I think this one was
done on a relatively
inexpensive, smooth
100gsm paper. I wanted
to build almost
photographic or oil-
painterly qualities
into the skin tones.
Penciling in all the
body tones helped
to keep this figure
believably
physical.

The cyborg, jack-
hammer spikers
were drawn
separately.

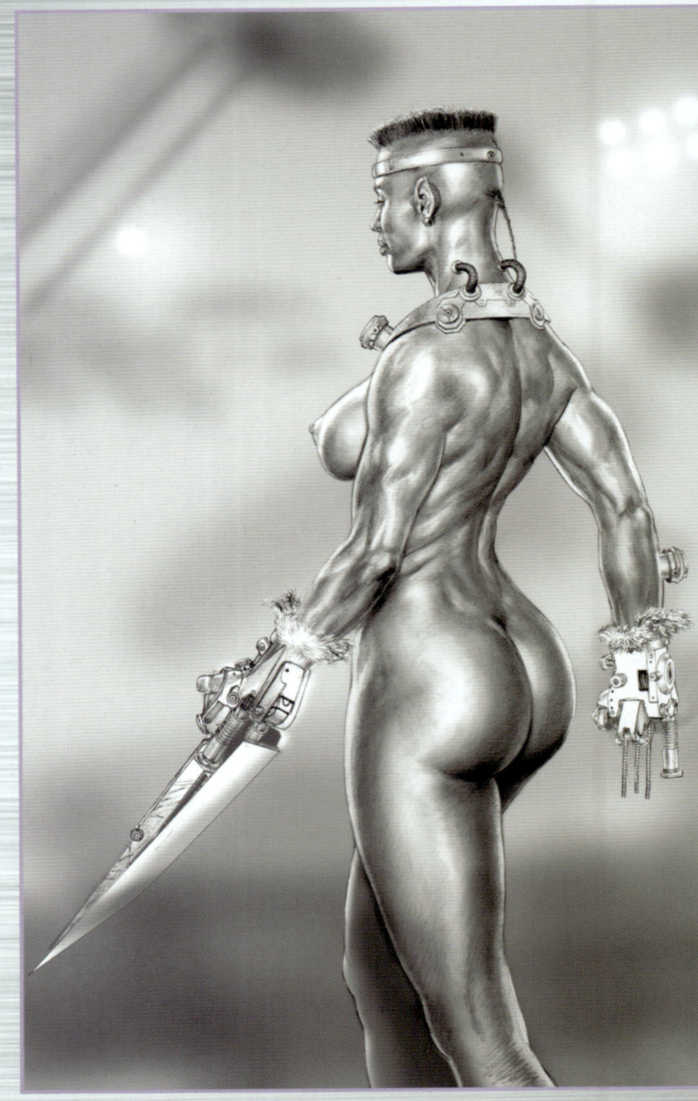

0263-Arena - Obelisk. This piece was done in tones almost through to
the end, because I was so unsure how I wanted to handle the colors. The
Cyborg Monster Robot-Killer is a crowd favorite at a futuristic Wrestling/
Monster Truck Rally, and she has just brought down a giant robot and
rests - one cybernetic retractable Piledriver spike has shattered - it was a
mechanical addition replacing her real hand! Eventually this will be part
of a quadriptych, and when I stitch them together, I'll embellish the
background too.

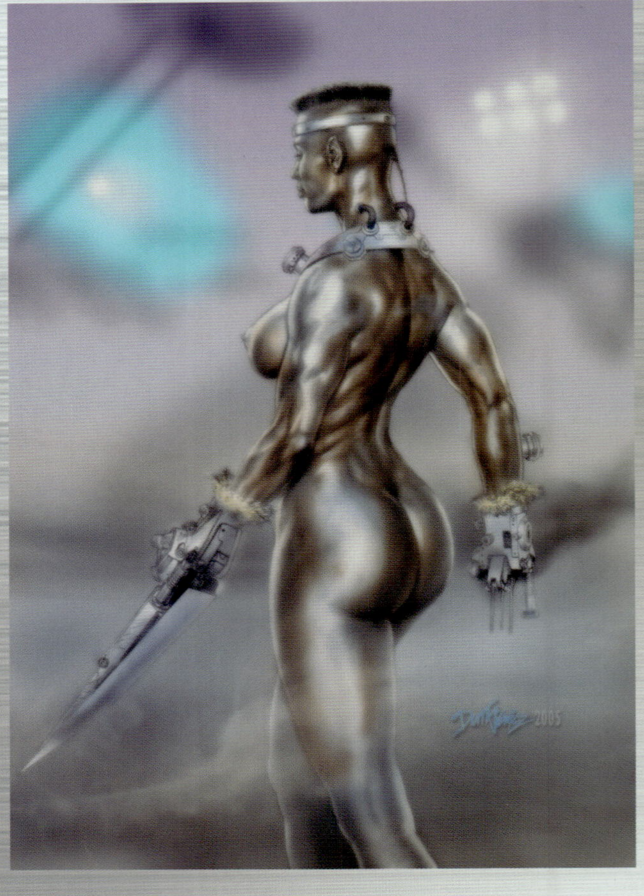

The funny thing on this double page spread is
that the same model posed for both images.

On this page I also referred to many photos of
female body-builders and also photographed a
small-built, but muscular, male Physical Trainer,
named Tak, who helped with background elements
in the recent Lost In Space project I worked on.
I found this a very difficult piece to do,
not just because the figure had to retain some
feminine characteristics, but because I had to
pose and direct both models so carefully.

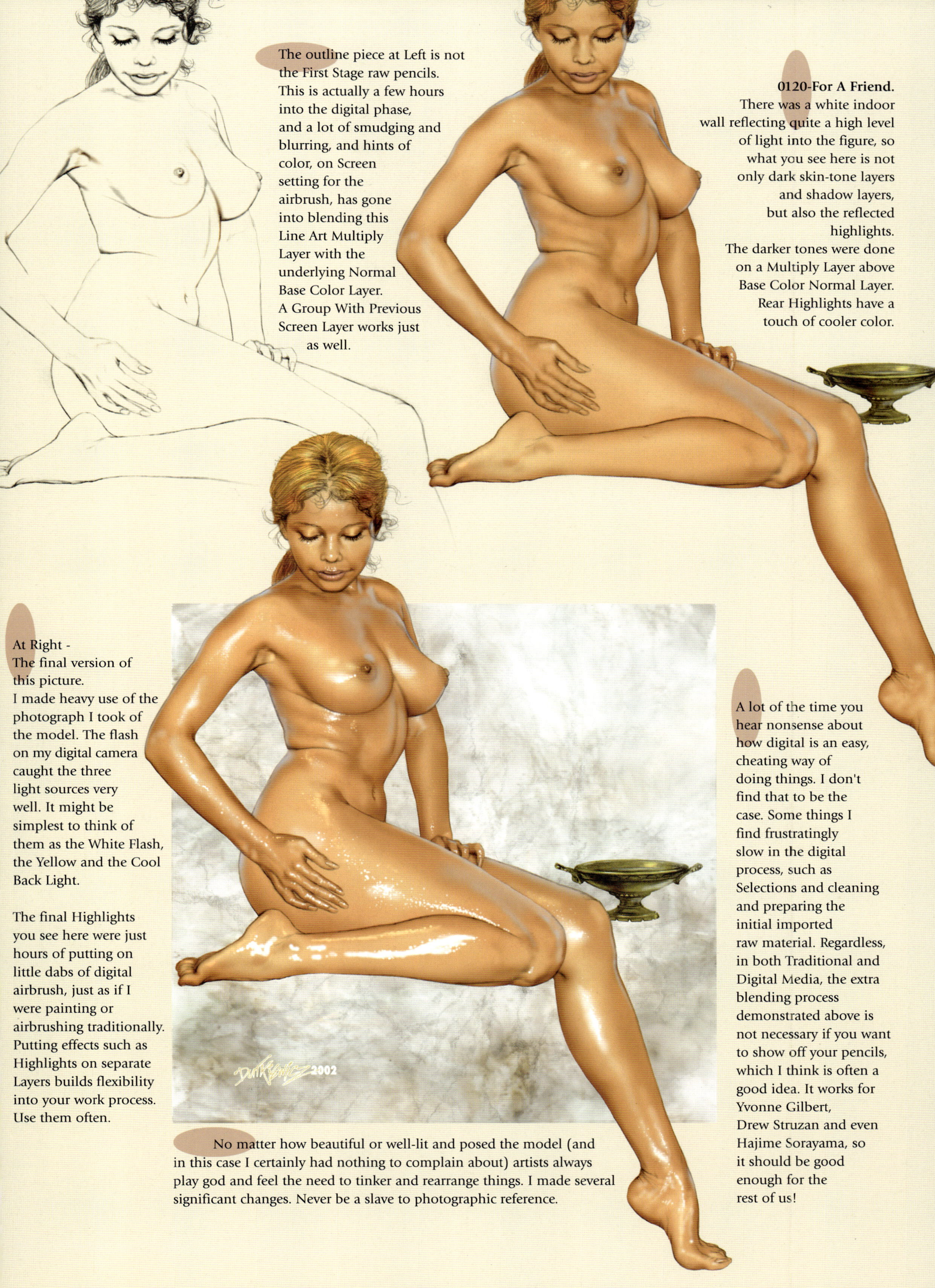

The outline piece at Left is not the First Stage raw pencils. This is actually a few hours into the digital phase, and a lot of smudging and blurring, and hints of color, on Screen setting for the airbrush, has gone into blending this Line Art Multiply Layer with the underlying Normal Base Color Layer. A Group With Previous Screen Layer works just as well.

0120-For A Friend.
There was a white indoor wall reflecting quite a high level of light into the figure, so what you see here is not only dark skin-tone layers and shadow layers, but also the reflected highlights. The darker tones were done on a Multiply Layer above Base Color Normal Layer. Rear Highlights have a touch of cooler color.

At Right -
The final version of this picture.
I made heavy use of the photograph I took of the model. The flash on my digital camera caught the three light sources very well. It might be simplest to think of them as the White Flash, the Yellow and the Cool Back Light.

The final Highlights you see here were just hours of putting on little dabs of digital airbrush, just as if I were painting or airbrushing traditionally. Putting effects such as Highlights on separate Layers builds flexibility into your work process. Use them often.

A lot of the time you hear nonsense about how digital is an easy, cheating way of doing things. I don't find that to be the case. Some things I find frustratingly slow in the digital process, such as Selections and cleaning and preparing the initial imported raw material. Regardless, in both Traditional and Digital Media, the extra blending process demonstrated above is not necessary if you want to show off your pencils, which I think is often a good idea. It works for Yvonne Gilbert, Drew Struzan and even Hajime Sorayama, so it should be good enough for the rest of us!

No matter how beautiful or well-lit and posed the model (and in this case I certainly had nothing to complain about) artists always play god and feel the need to tinker and rearrange things. I made several significant changes. Never be a slave to photographic reference.

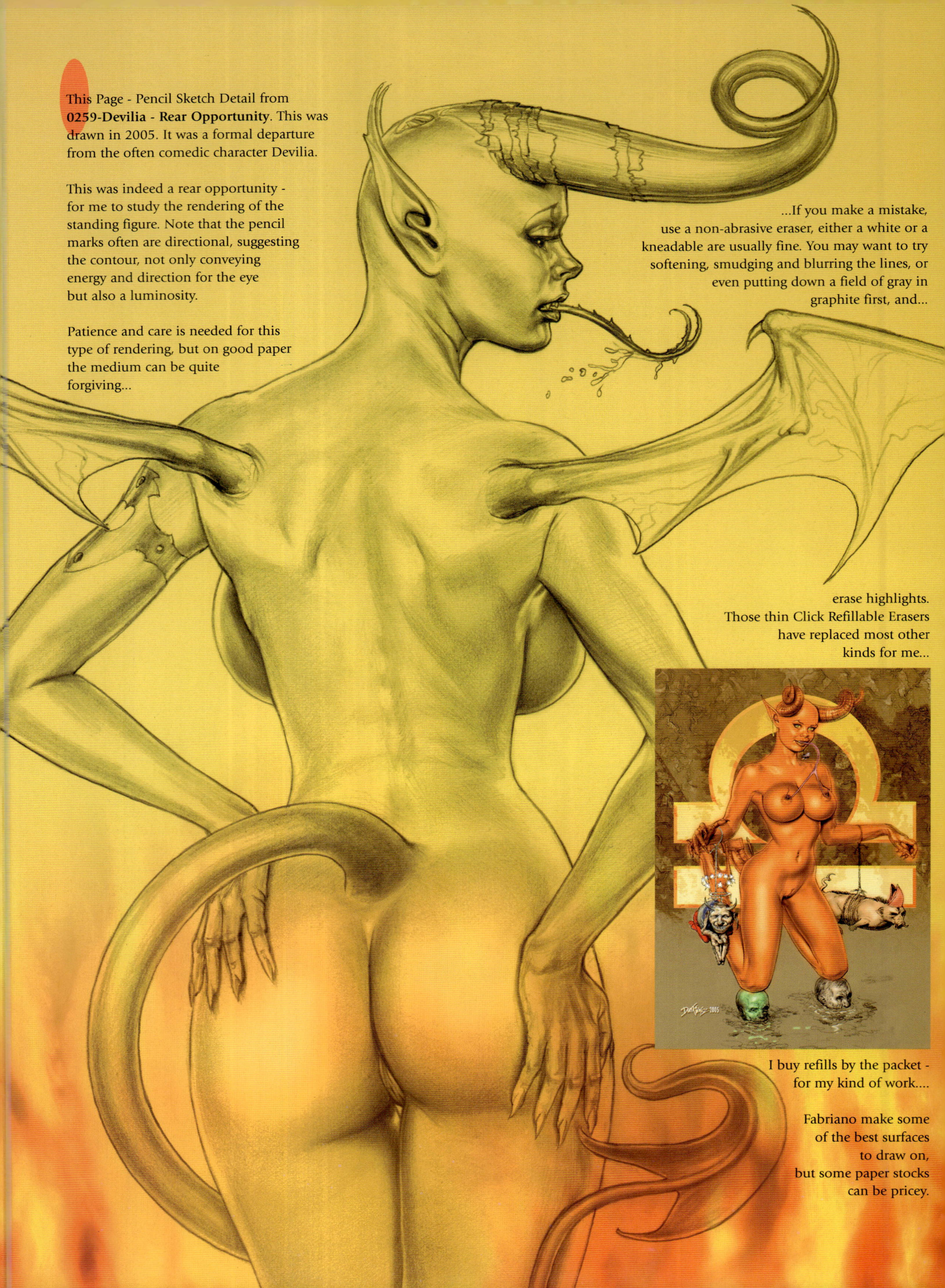

This Page - Pencil Sketch Detail from **0259-Devilia - Rear Opportunity**. This was drawn in 2005. It was a formal departure from the often comedic character Devilia.

This was indeed a rear opportunity - for me to study the rendering of the standing figure. Note that the pencil marks often are directional, suggesting the contour, not only conveying energy and direction for the eye but also a luminosity.

Patience and care is needed for this type of rendering, but on good paper the medium can be quite forgiving...

...If you make a mistake, use a non-abrasive eraser, either a white or a kneadable are usually fine. You may want to try softening, smudging and blurring the lines, or even putting down a field of gray in graphite first, and...

erase highlights. Those thin Click Refillable Erasers have replaced most other kinds for me...

I buy refills by the packet - for my kind of work....

Fabriano make some of the best surfaces to draw on, but some paper stocks can be pricey.

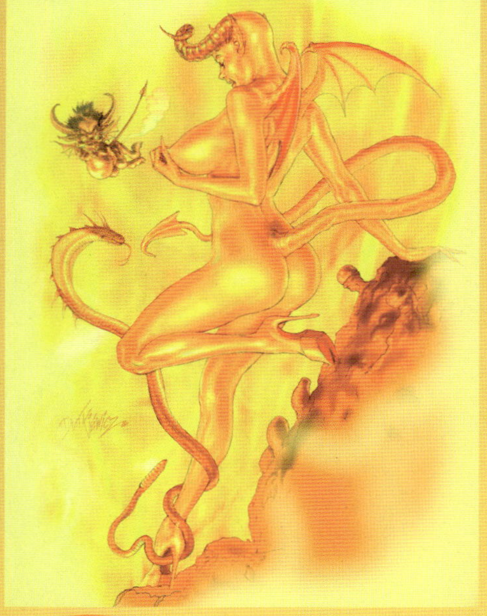

Above - 0050-Devilia 02 - Mesmerizing
Right -
0223-Devilia - Positively Tepid

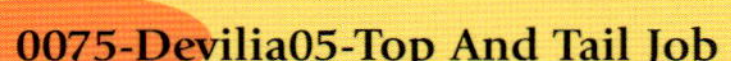

0075-Devilia05-Top And Tail Job

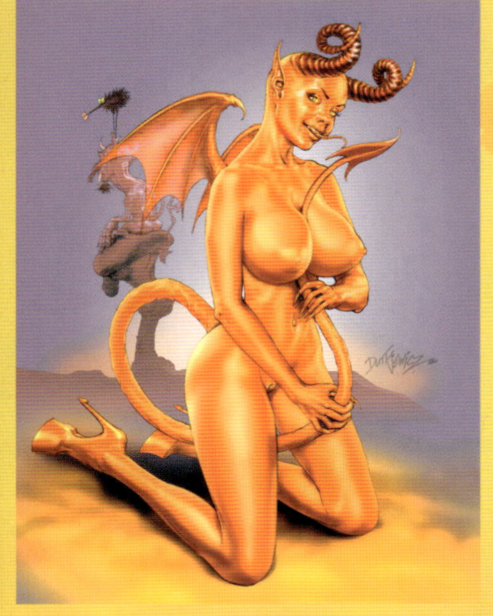

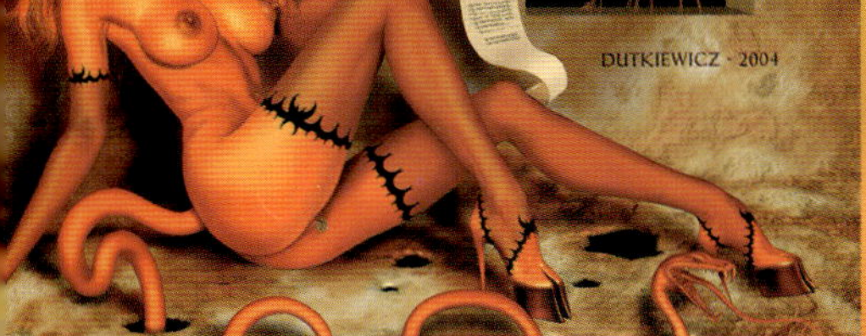

0242-Devilia - The Contract

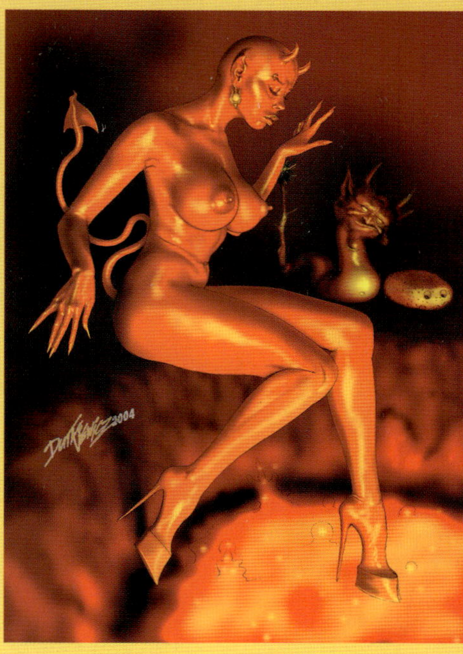

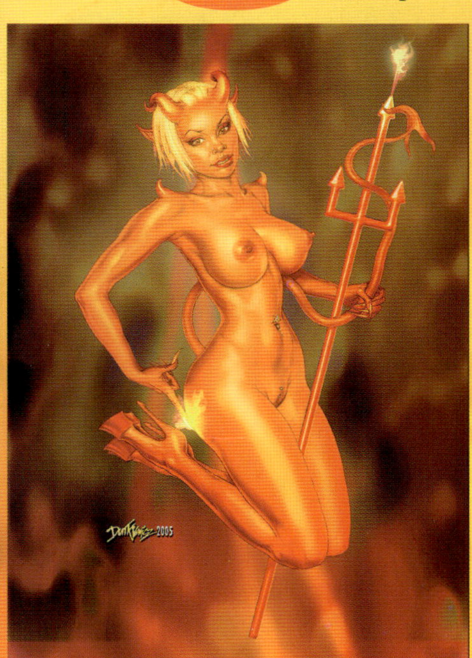

DEVILIA - is a chameleon... some Elements of her appearance are always changing or disappearing... ...except her cute face, wild, cloven, high-heeled feet and huge breasts!

0251-Devilia - Hotpoint

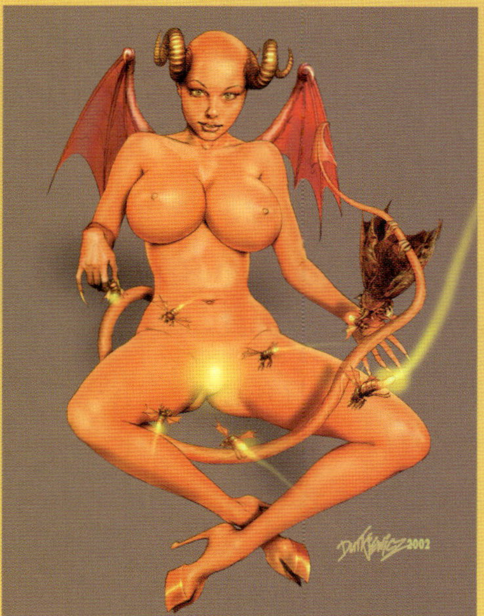

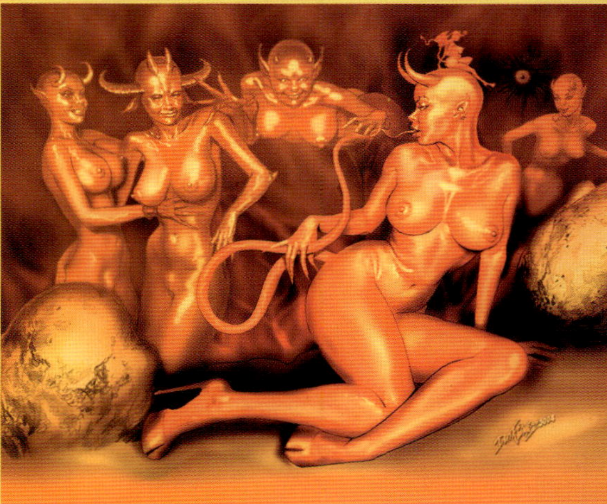

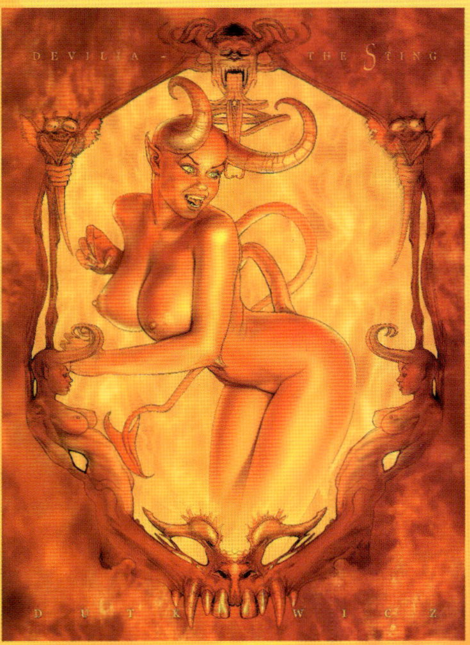

Top -
0hc-0007-Devilia07 - Pet Food.
Middle -
Almost complete Stage 5 of
0234-Devilia-Eternal Showtime.
Bottom -
0285-Devilia - The Sting.

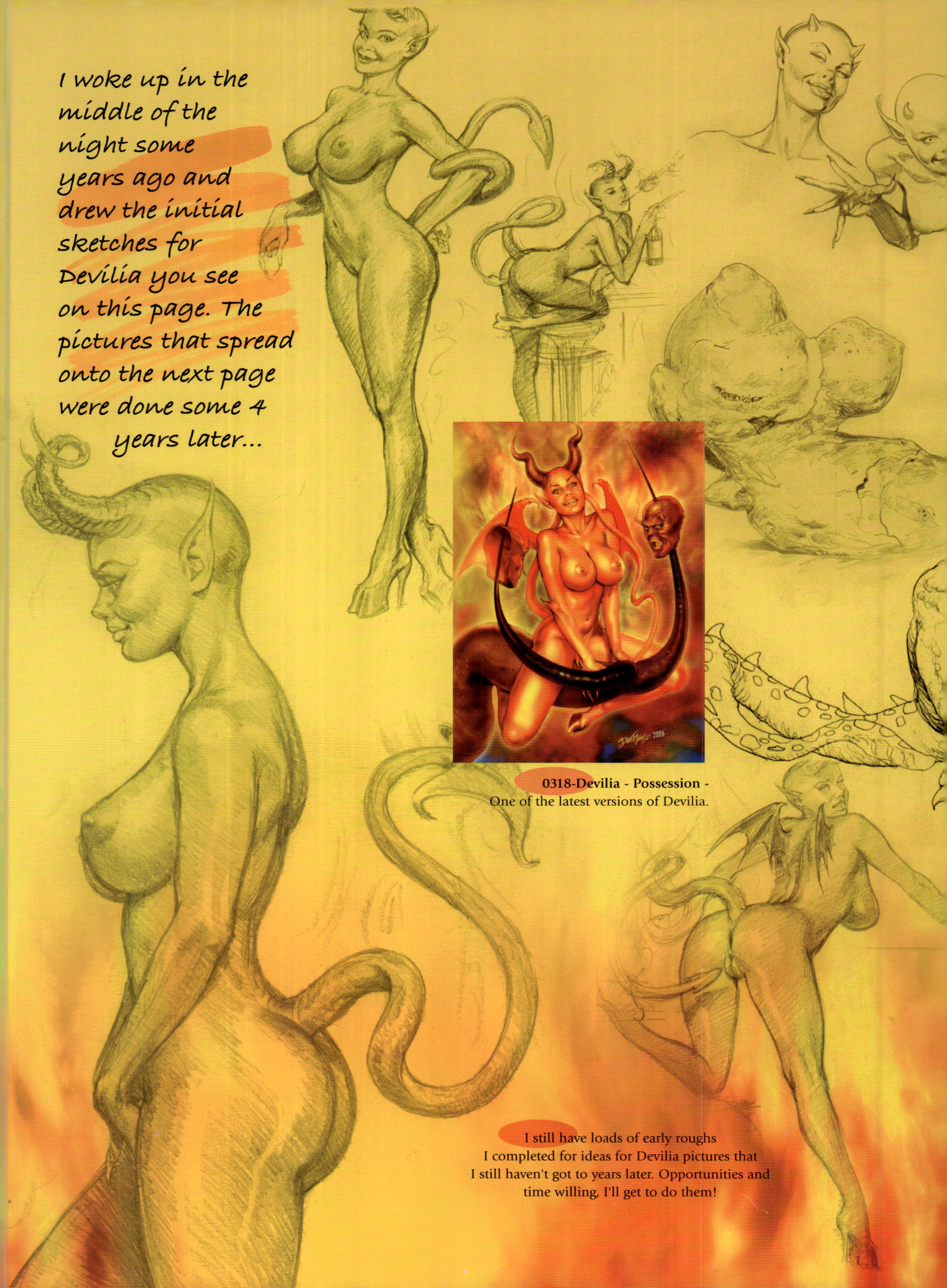

I woke up in the middle of the night some years ago and drew the initial sketches for Devilia you see on this page. The pictures that spread onto the next page were done some 4 years later...

0318-Devilia - Possession -
One of the latest versions of Devilia.

I still have loads of early roughs I completed for ideas for Devilia pictures that I still haven't got to years later. Opportunities and time willing, I'll get to do them!

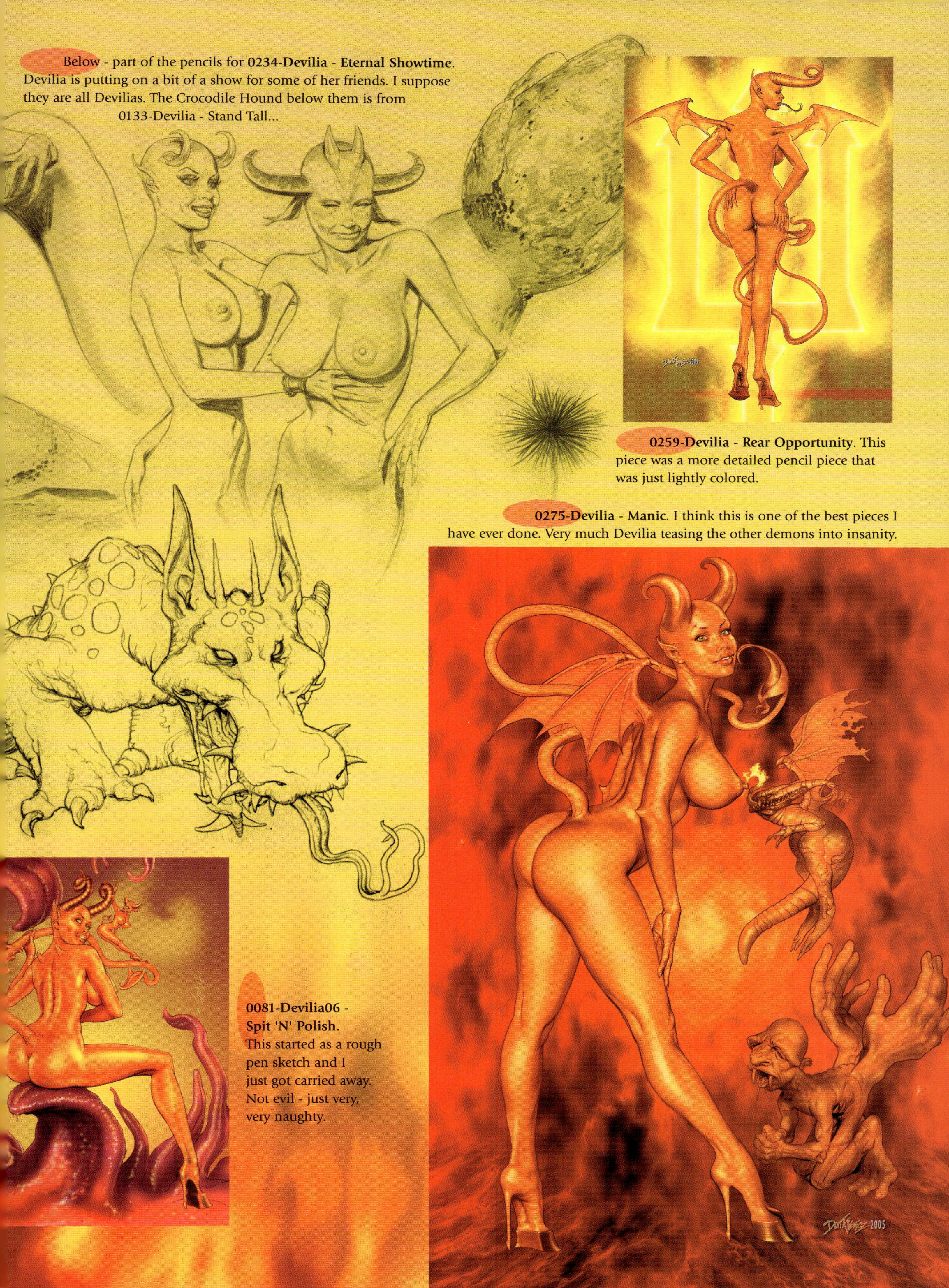

Below - part of the pencils for **0234-Devilia - Eternal Showtime**. Devilia is putting on a bit of a show for some of her friends. I suppose they are all Devilias. The Crocodile Hound below them is from 0133-Devilia - Stand Tall...

0259-Devilia - Rear Opportunity. This piece was a more detailed pencil piece that was just lightly colored.

0275-Devilia - Manic. I think this is one of the best pieces I have ever done. Very much Devilia teasing the other demons into insanity.

0081-Devilia06 - Spit 'N' Polish. This started as a rough pen sketch and I just got carried away. Not evil - just very, very naughty.

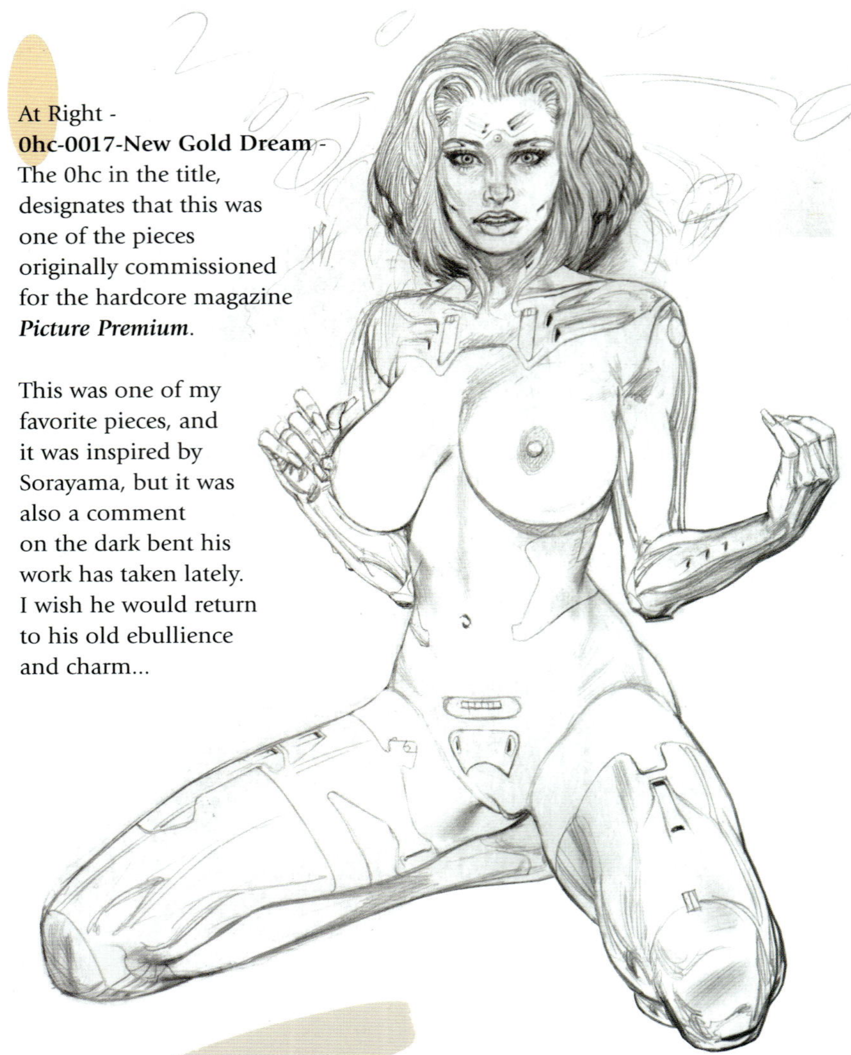

At Right -
0hc-0017-New Gold Dream -
The 0hc in the title,
designates that this was
one of the pieces
originally commissioned
for the hardcore magazine
Picture Premium.

This was one of my
favorite pieces, and
it was inspired by
Sorayama, but it was
also a comment
on the dark bent his
work has taken lately.
I wish he would return
to his old ebullience
and charm...

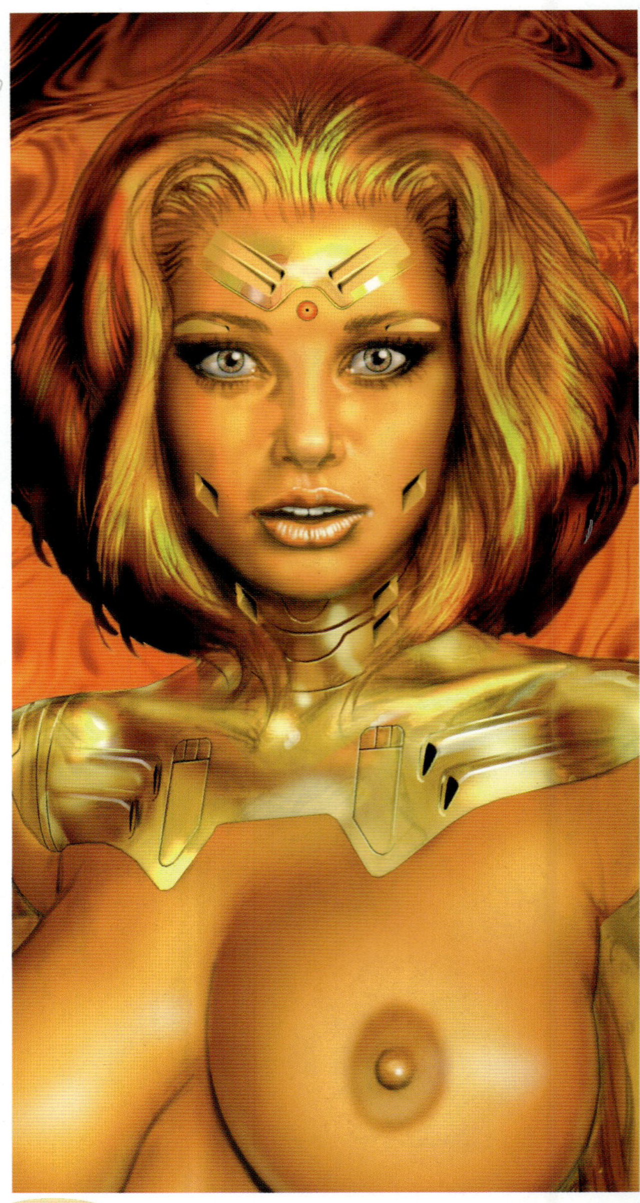

*At the time I produced this picture, I was
taking every chance I could to perfect my
technique and increase my knowledge...
...I am more into enjoying the process now...*

Above - the rough sketch at right has had many careful
masks and elements added from Photoshop fabrications -
notice especially the vents, eyes, and chrome areas.

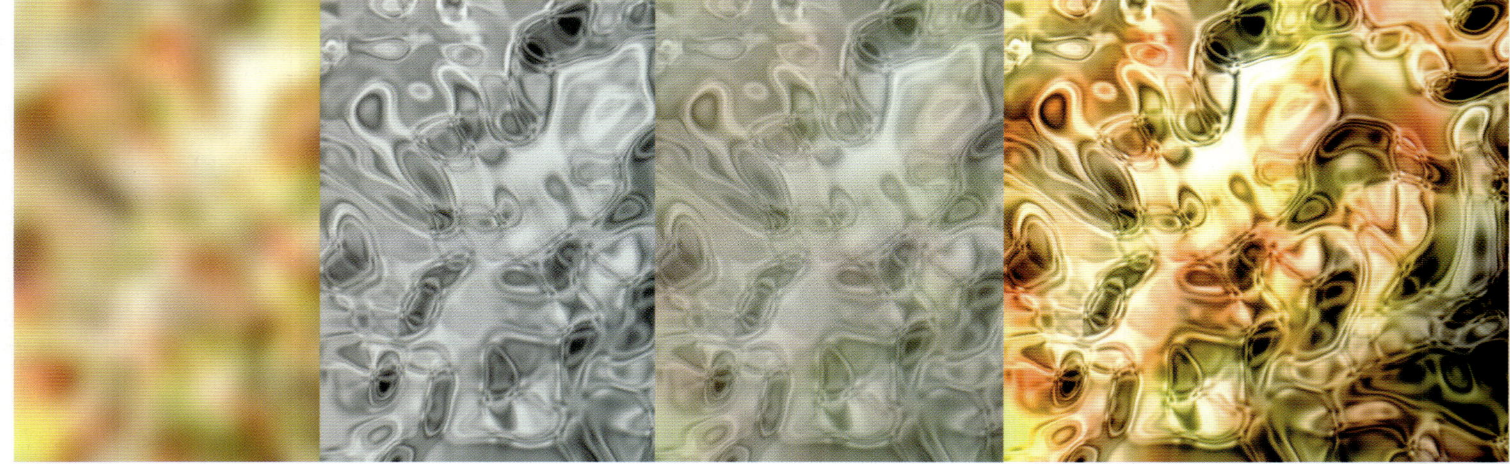

Above - This is a simple effect to create in Adobe Photoshop. Simply fill a layer with white or a tone or hue, then spray some colors with a
blurry brush, or generate a field using the HSB Noise Filter in Eye Candy - one of the most superb Plug-Ins for Photoshop. Next, go to the
Filter Menu/Sketch/Chrome and apply the Chrome so that it is relatively Smooth and Detail is relatively low. Then go straight to the Edit
Menu/Fade and slide the bar down until the colors just start to re-emerge. Finally, play with the Brightness/Contrast settings in the
Image/Adjust/Brightness/Contrast Menu and play with the Dodge and Burn Tools, possibly Burning Midtones and Dodging set on
Highlights with a wide, soft-edged brush. I use the Fade option extensively to create subtlety, even when just using the Airbrush Tool etc.

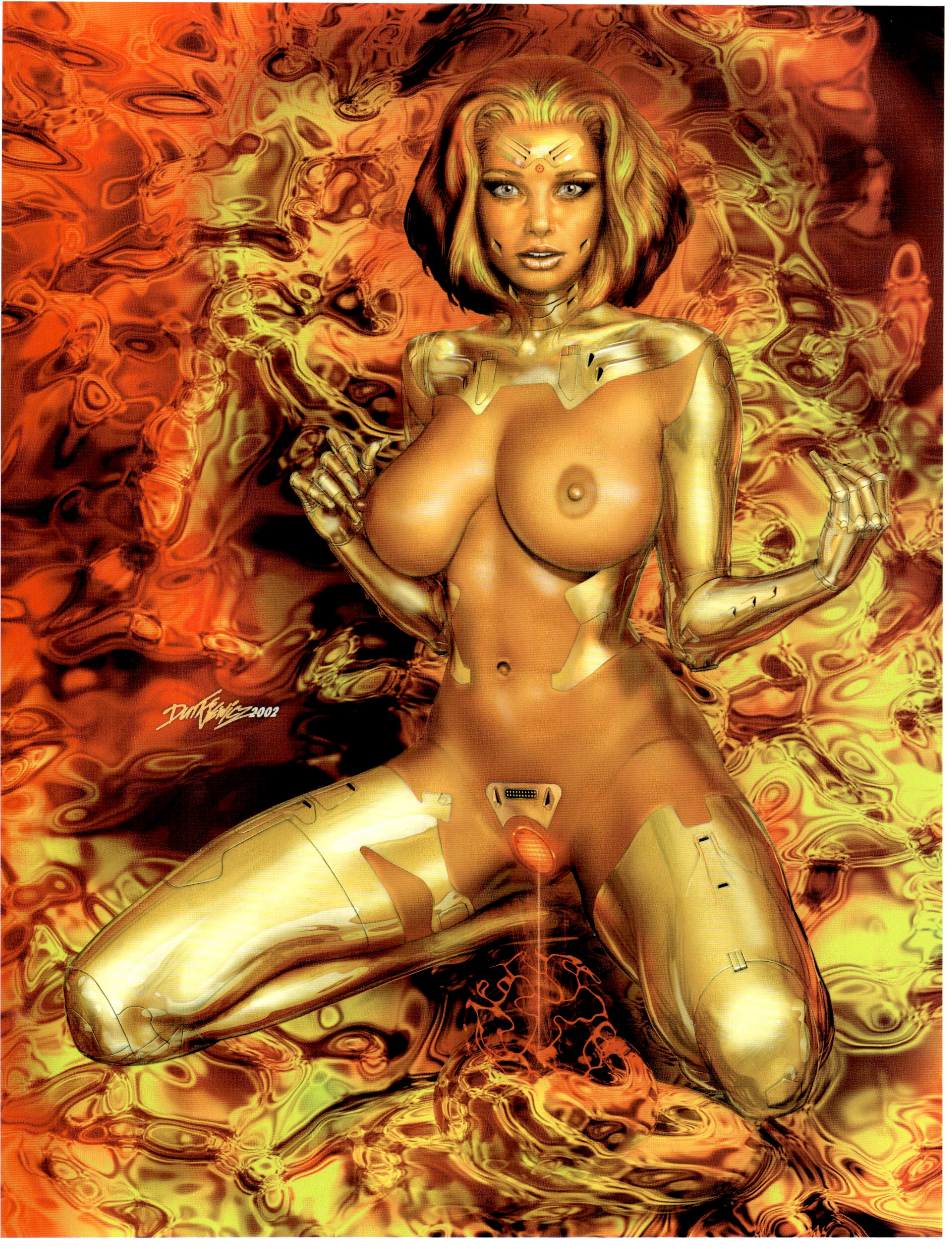

Sorry! I apologize for telling
people there was to be a poster of
this piece to be coming out
soon. That deal fell by the roadside
but we are still trying.
People keep asking me if
posters are available, but
I am not massively
entrepreneurial and I find
it hard to find time for such
things, but if I
can free up some time,
I'll definitely consider
a series.

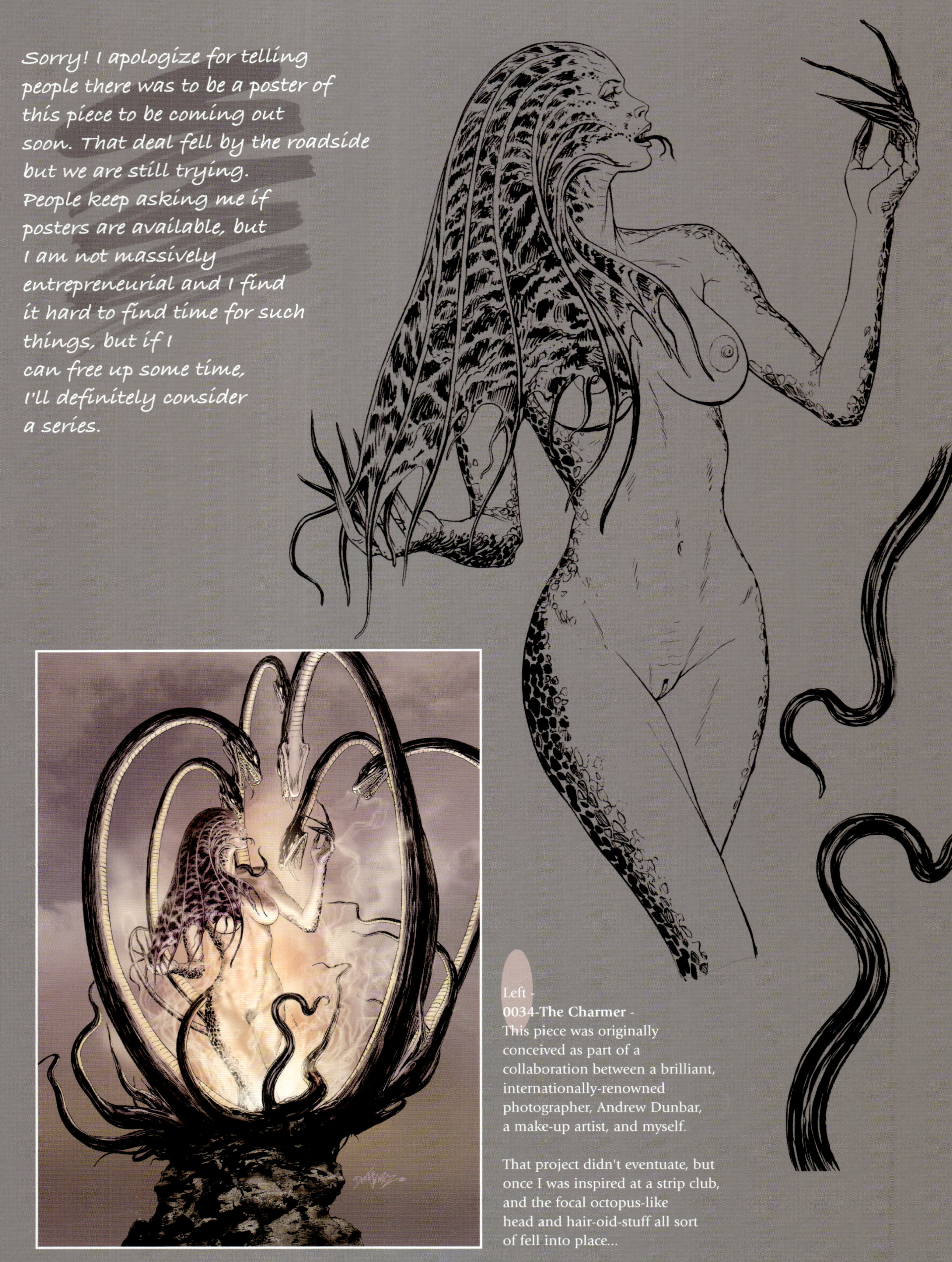

Left -
0034-The Charmer -
This piece was originally
conceived as part of a
collaboration between a brilliant,
internationally-renowned
photographer, Andrew Dunbar,
a make-up artist, and myself.

That project didn't eventuate, but
once I was inspired at a strip club,
and the focal octopus-like
head and hair-oid-stuff all sort
of fell into place...

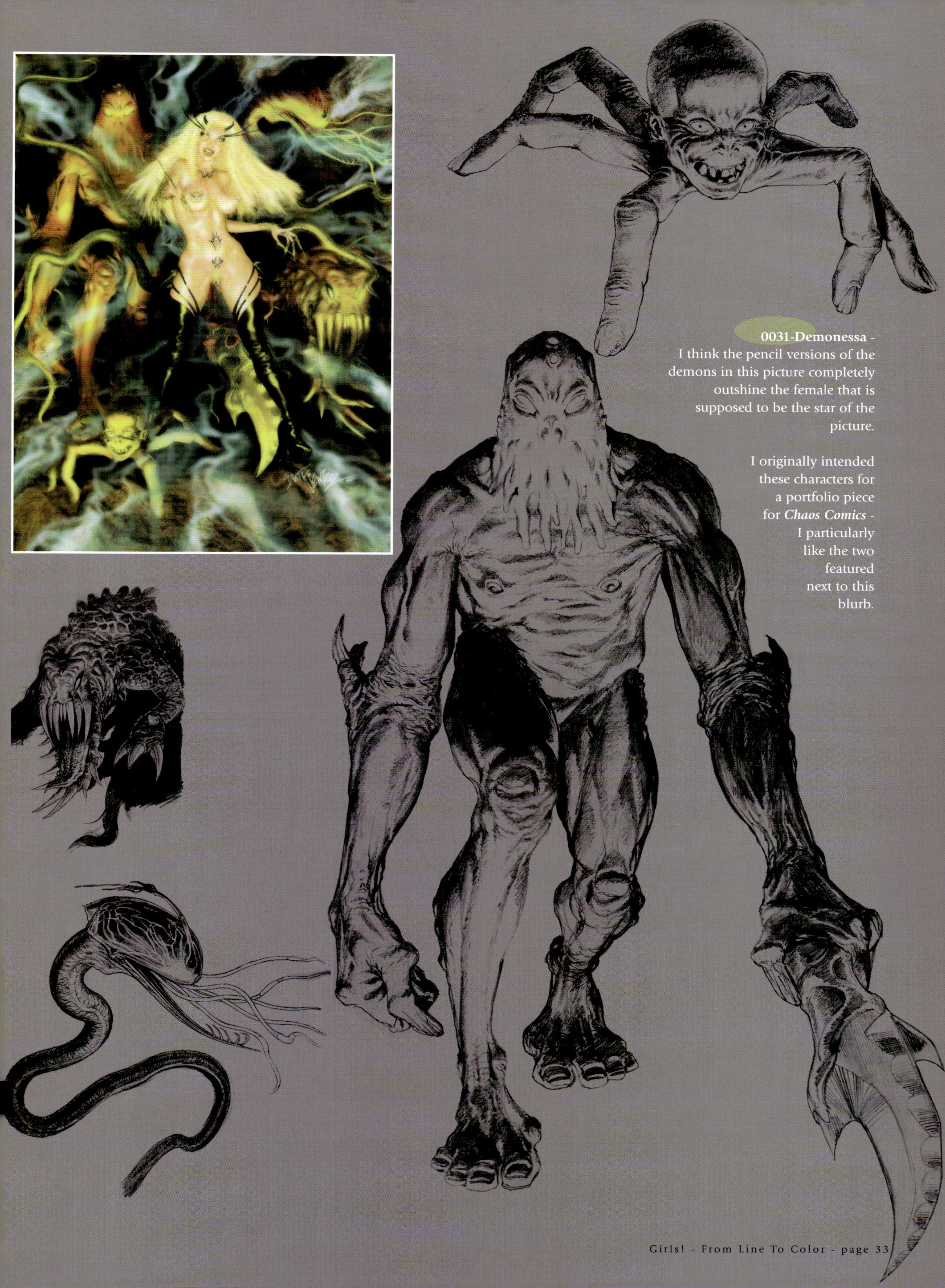

0031-Demonessa -
I think the pencil versions of the demons in this picture completely outshine the female that is supposed to be the star of the picture.

I originally intended these characters for a portfolio piece for *Chaos Comics* - I particularly like the two featured next to this blurb.

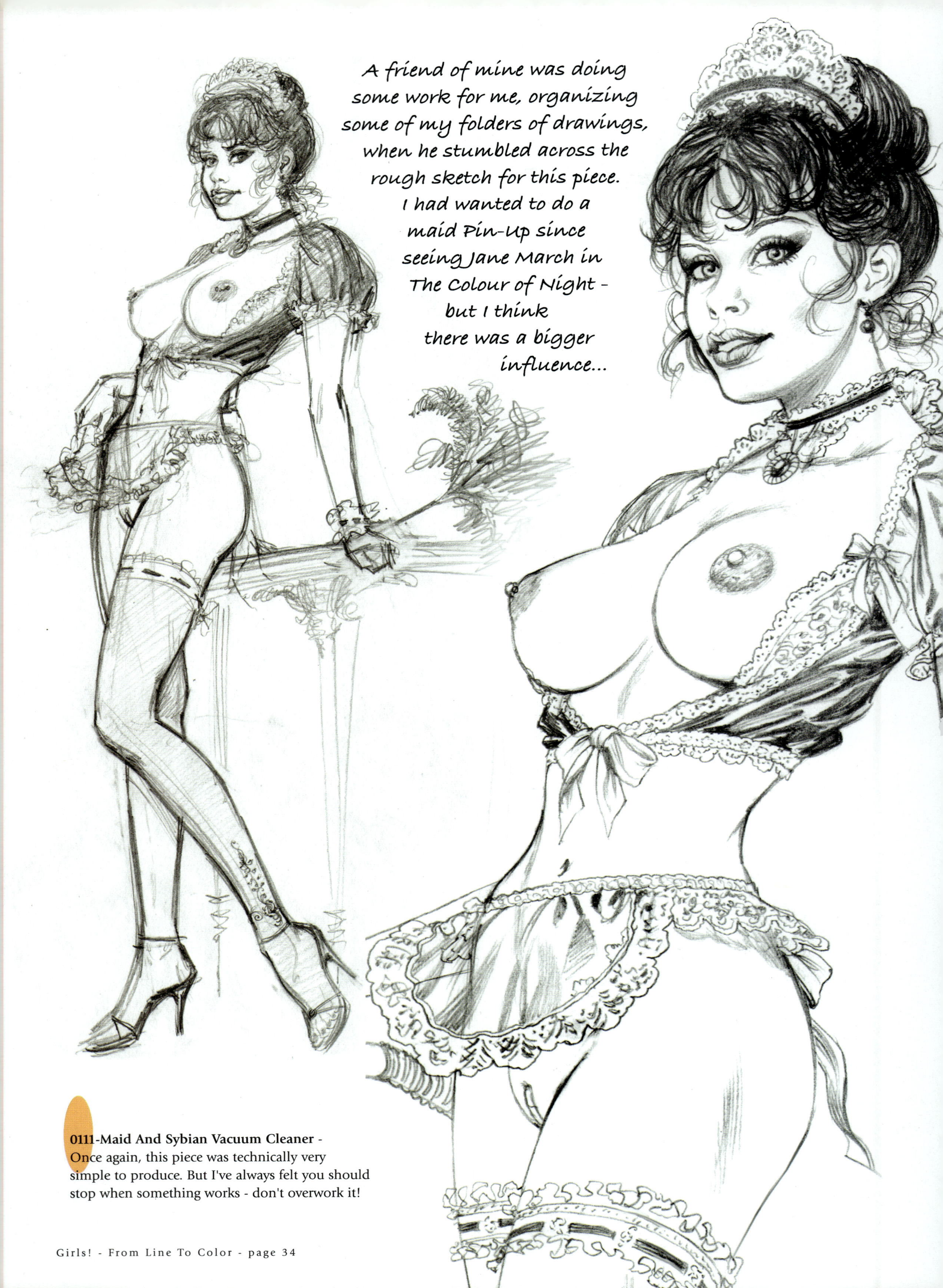

0111-Maid And Sybian Vacuum Cleaner - Once again, this piece was technically very simple to produce. But I've always felt you should stop when something works - don't overwork it!

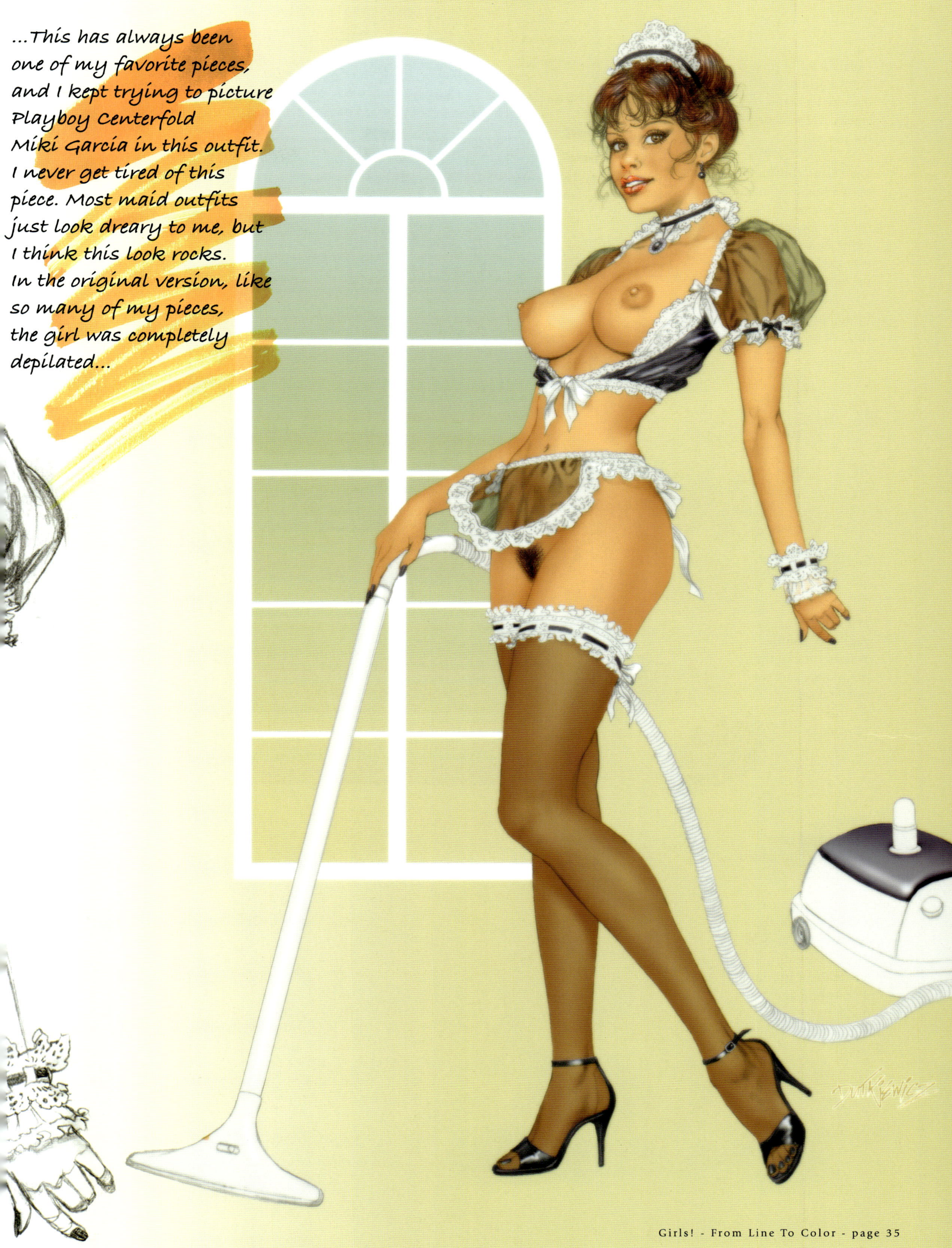

...This has always been one of my favorite pieces, and I kept trying to picture Playboy Centerfold Miki Garcia in this outfit. I never get tired of this piece. Most maid outfits just look dreary to me, but I think this look rocks. In the original version, like so many of my pieces, the girl was completely depilated...

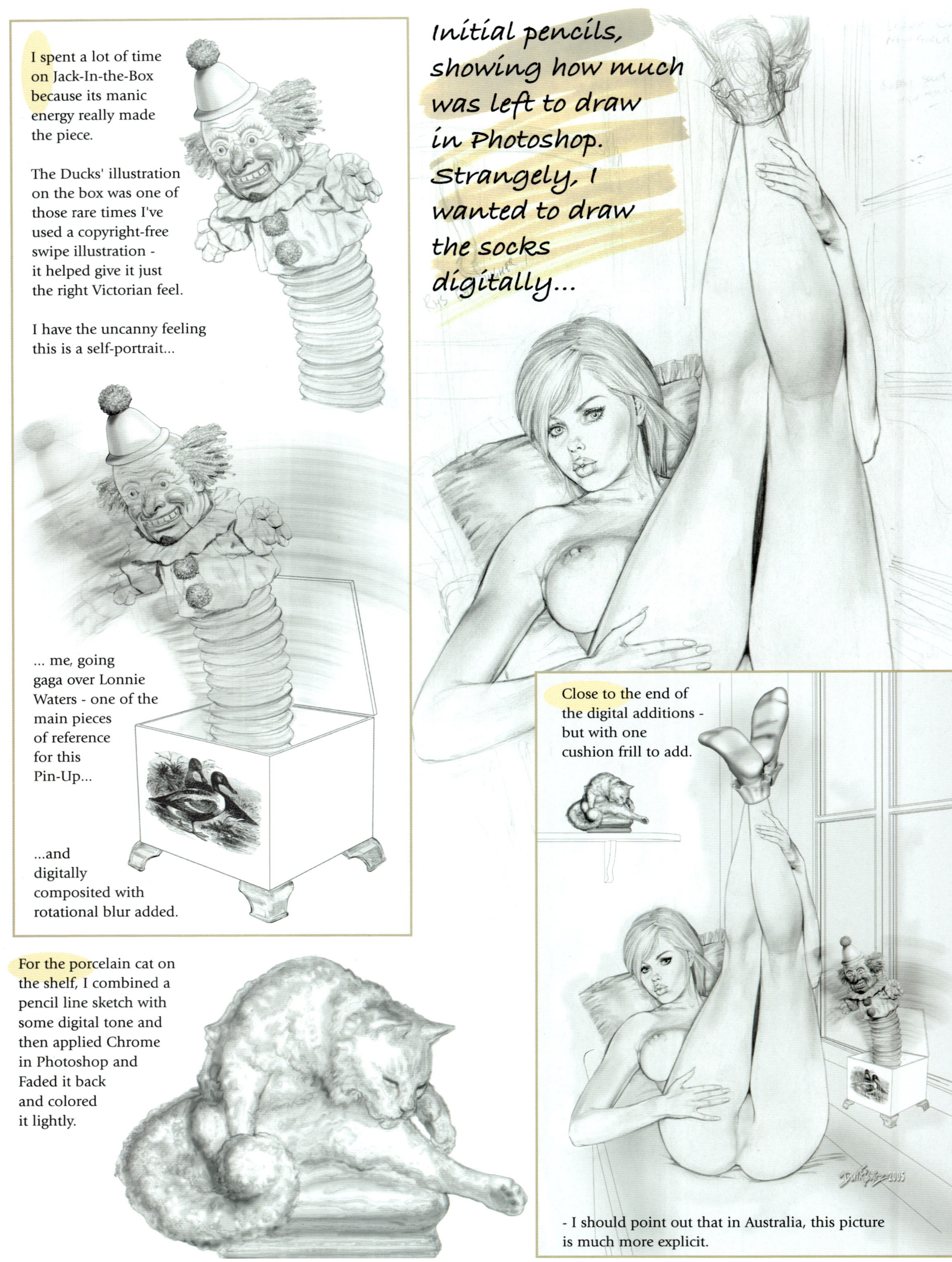

I spent a lot of time on Jack-In-the-Box because its manic energy really made the piece.

The Ducks' illustration on the box was one of those rare times I've used a copyright-free swipe illustration - it helped give it just the right Victorian feel.

I have the uncanny feeling this is a self-portrait...

... me, going gaga over Lonnie Waters - one of the main pieces of reference for this Pin-Up...

...and digitally composited with rotational blur added.

For the porcelain cat on the shelf, I combined a pencil line sketch with some digital tone and then applied Chrome in Photoshop and Faded it back and colored it lightly.

Initial pencils, showing how much was left to draw in Photoshop. Strangely, I wanted to draw the socks digitally...

Close to the end of the digital additions - but with one cushion frill to add.

- I should point out that in Australia, this picture is much more explicit.

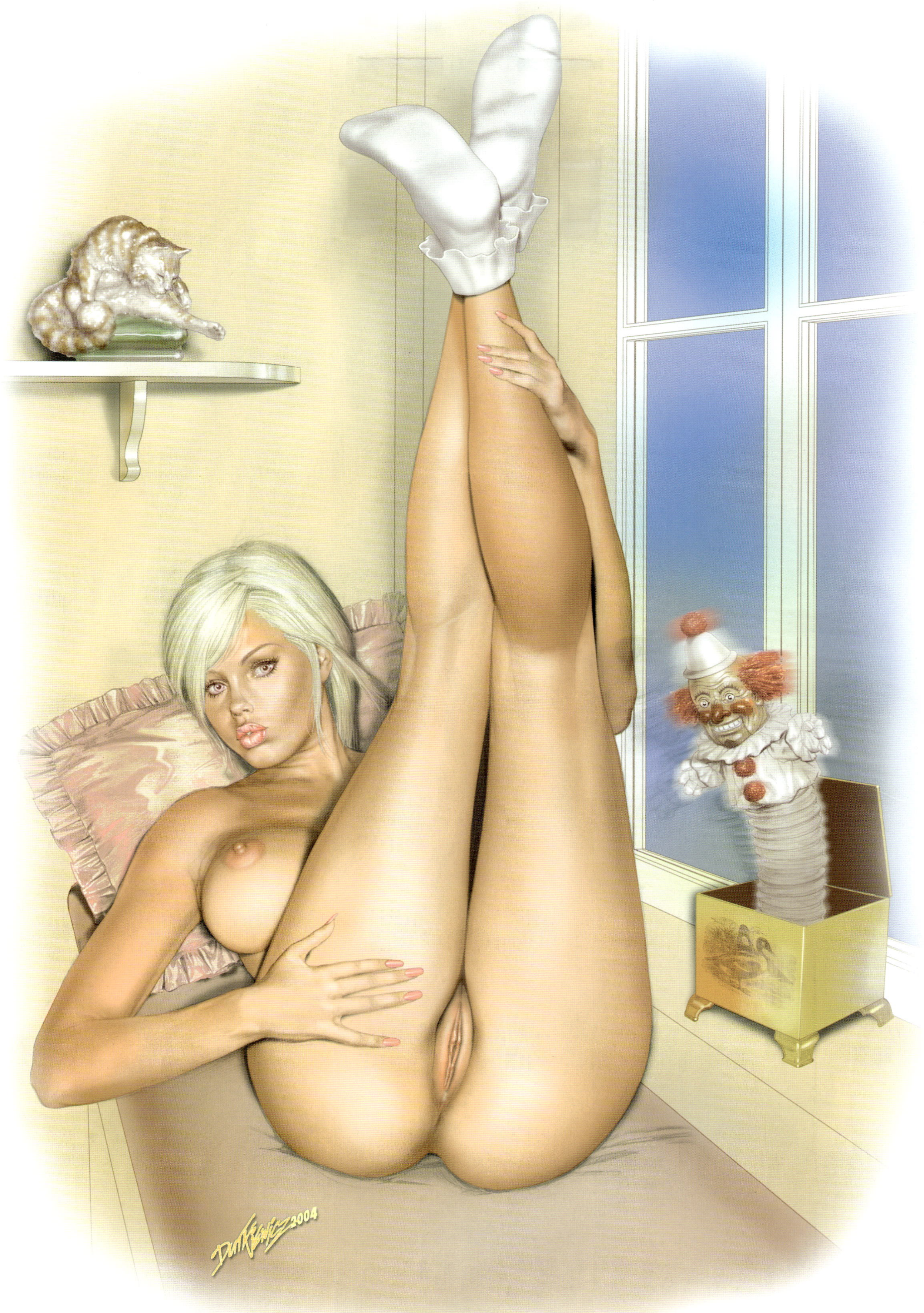

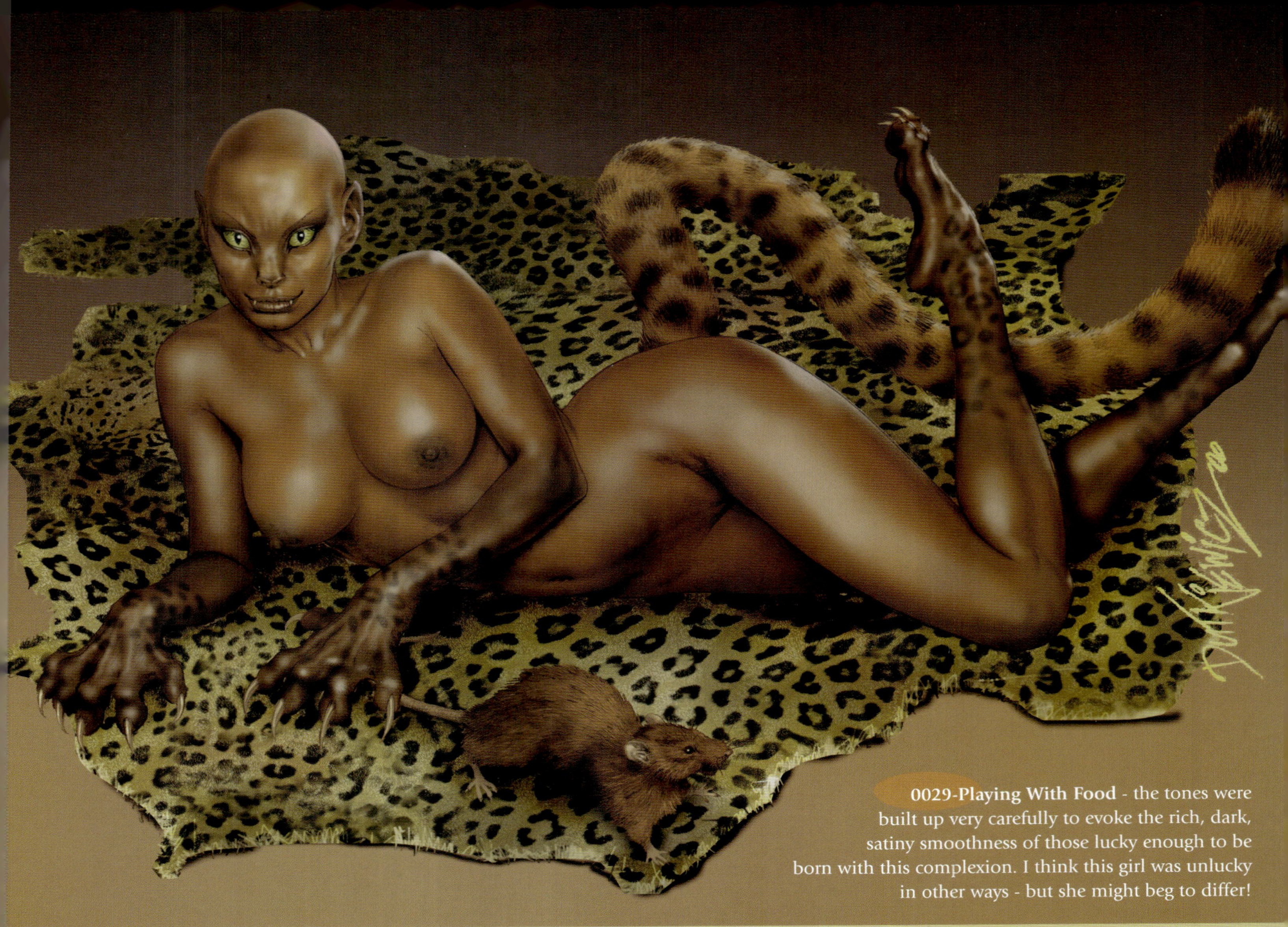

0029-Playing With Food - the tones were built up very carefully to evoke the rich, dark, satiny smoothness of those lucky enough to be born with this complexion. I think this girl was unlucky in other ways - but she might beg to differ!

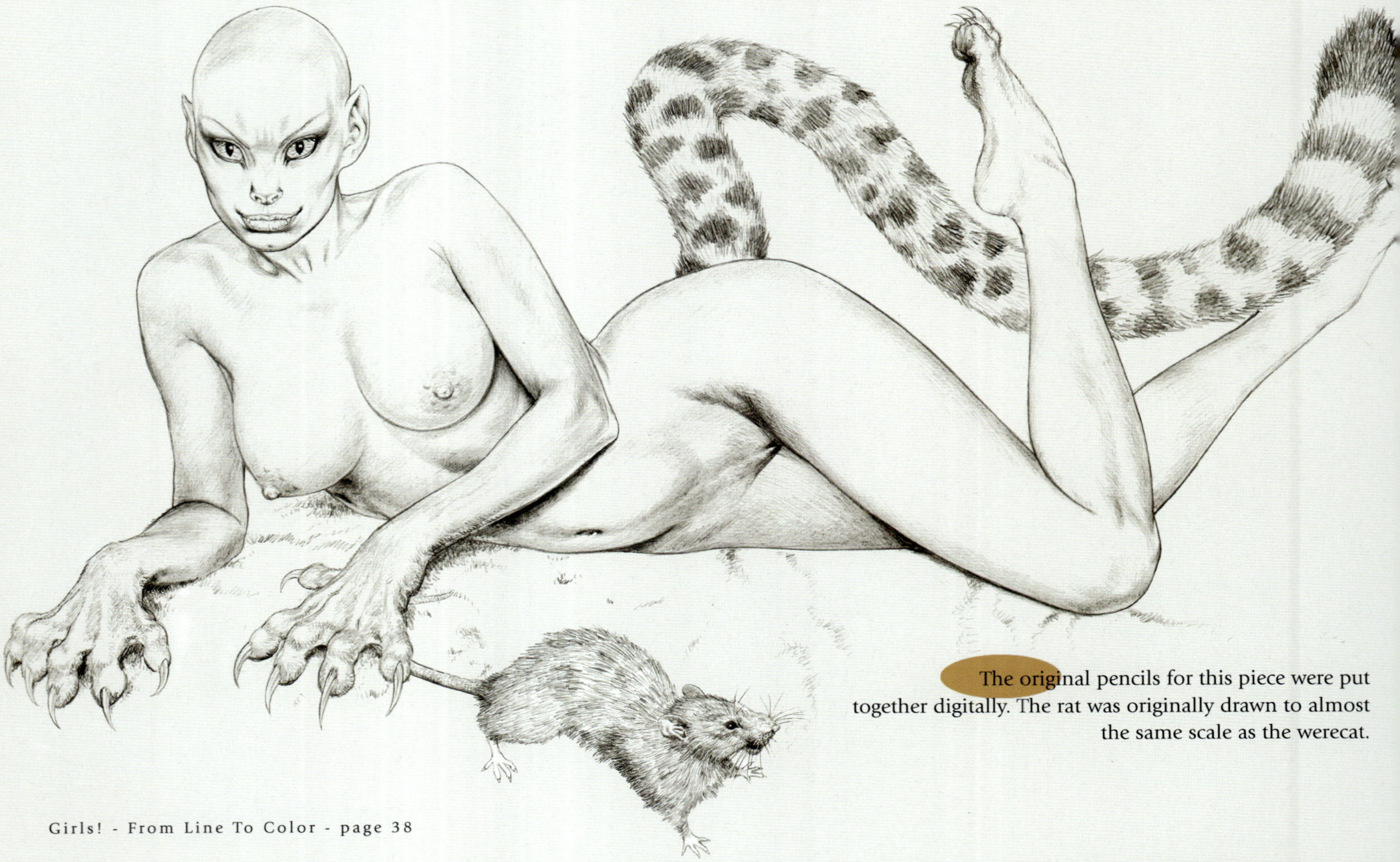

The original pencils for this piece were put together digitally. The rat was originally drawn to almost the same scale as the werecat.

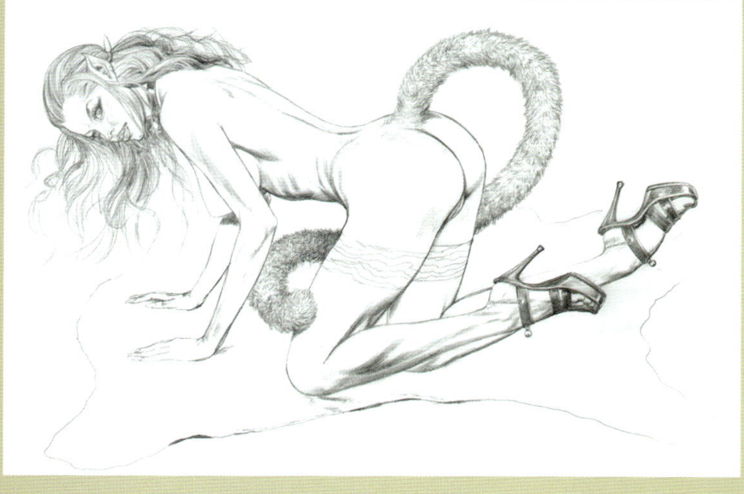
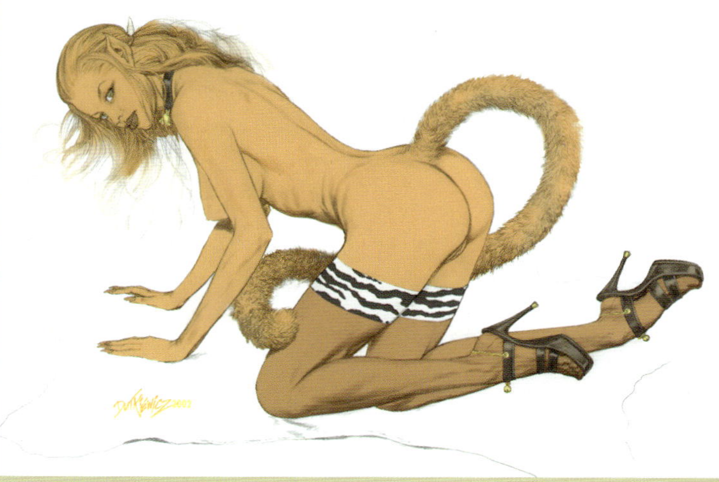

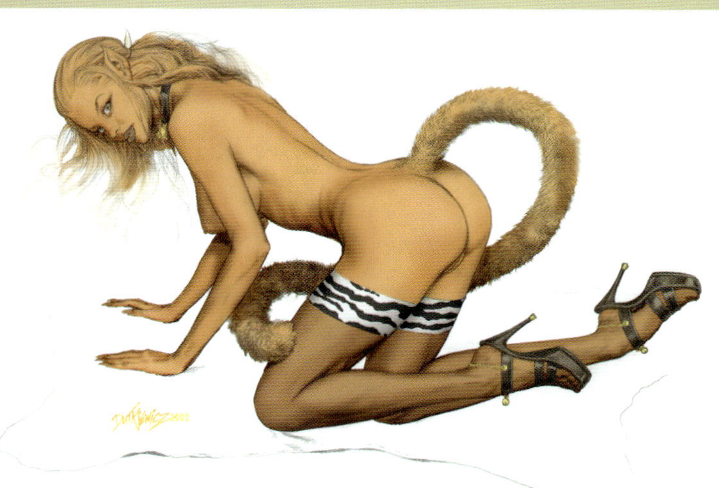
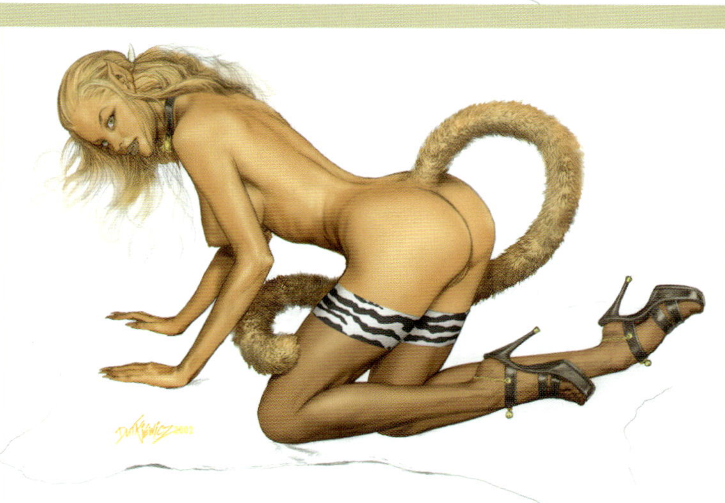

0105-Belling The Cat - this was one of the first times I began to simplify the content and concentrate on the impact of the image. The process involved putting the base colors in on one layer above the Background Layer; then building a Layer on Normal Mode for the base figure colors; then, above that, a layer in Multiply Blending Mode for Darks; then over that, a Screen Blending Mode Layer for lighter tones; and finally, above the Line Art Layer, a Layer for Highlights.

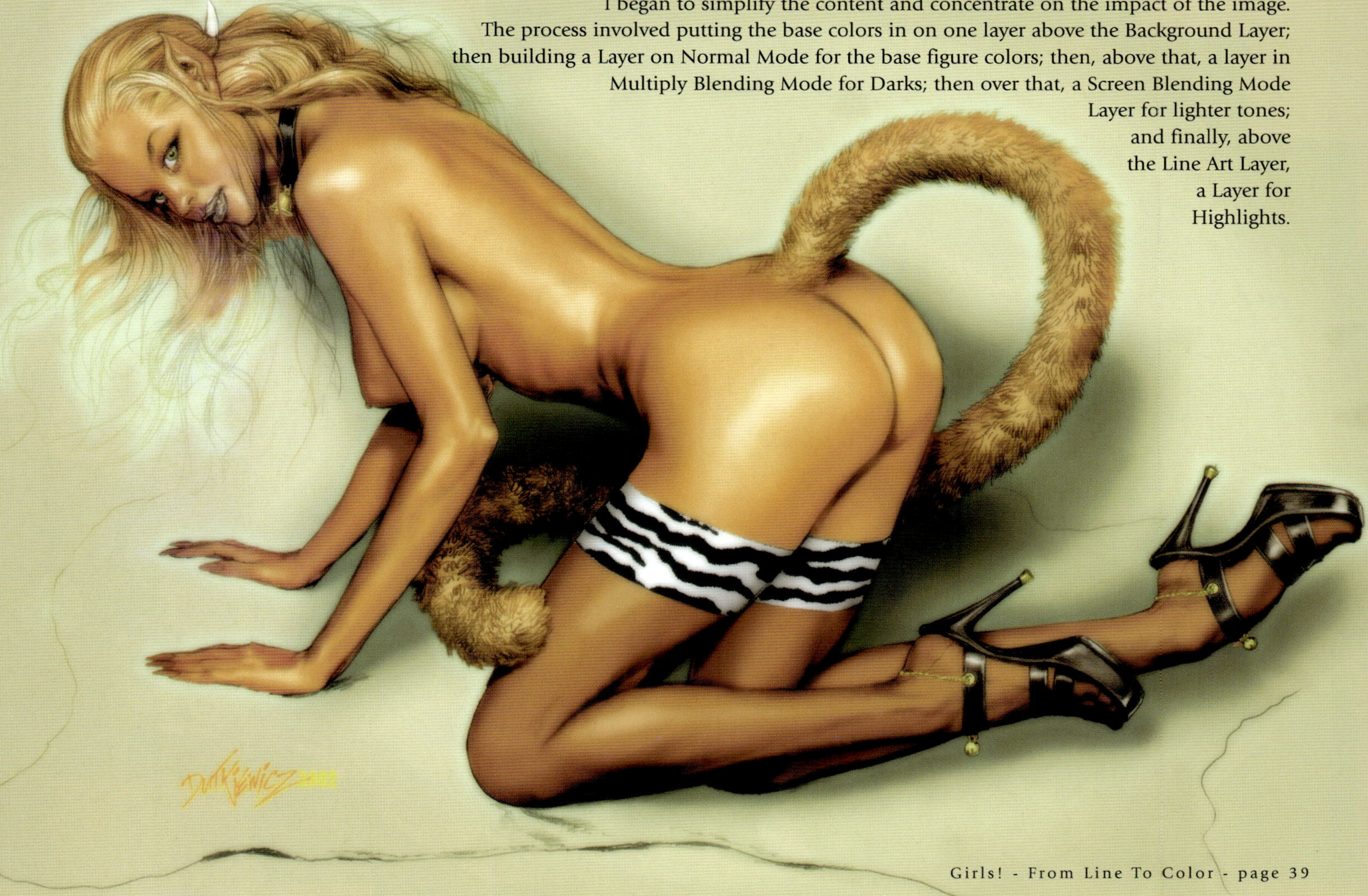

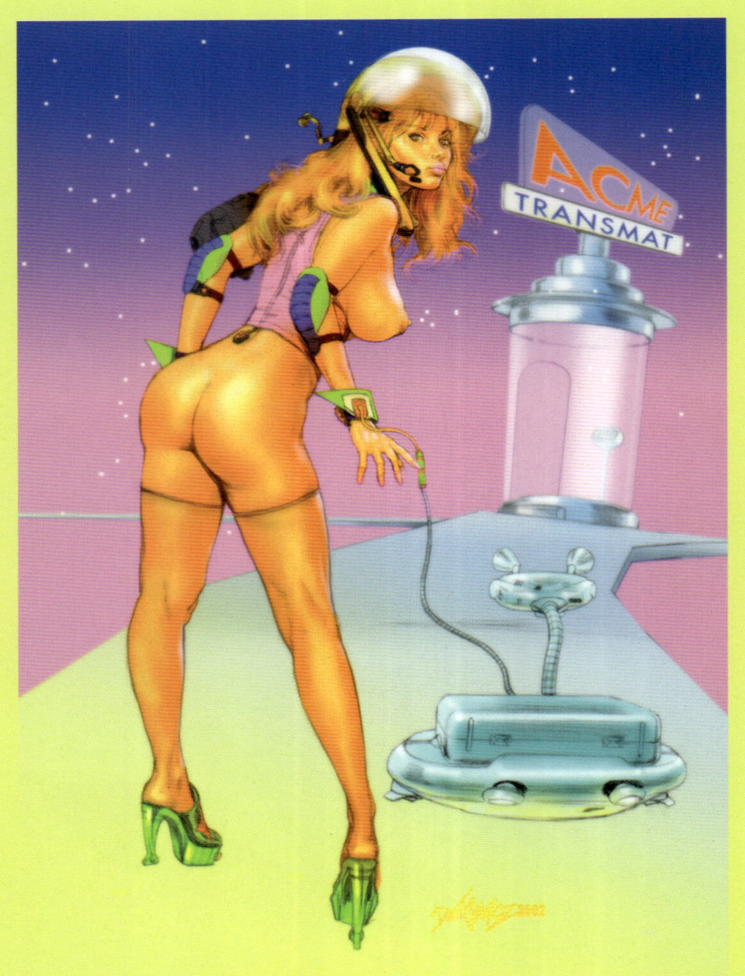

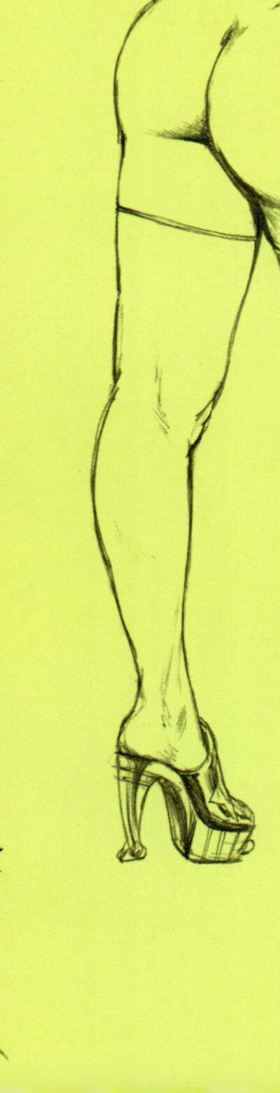

0087-Pet A Porter.
My favorite model helped out, yet again, with this brash, almost cartoony piece. The pencil pieces shown on this page show how much compositing and adding was done in the computer.

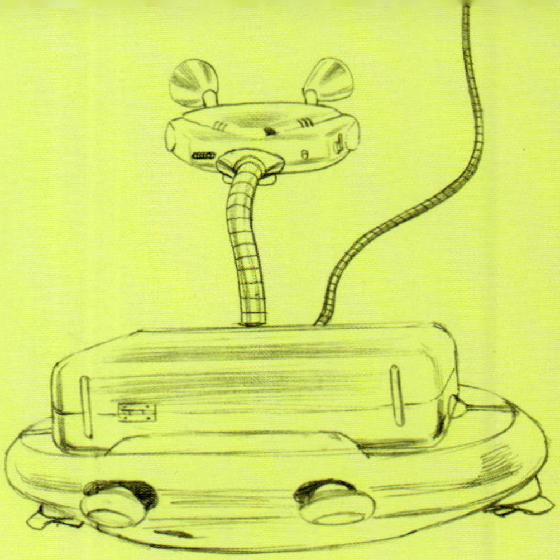

This one will be featured full-size in my next full color book.

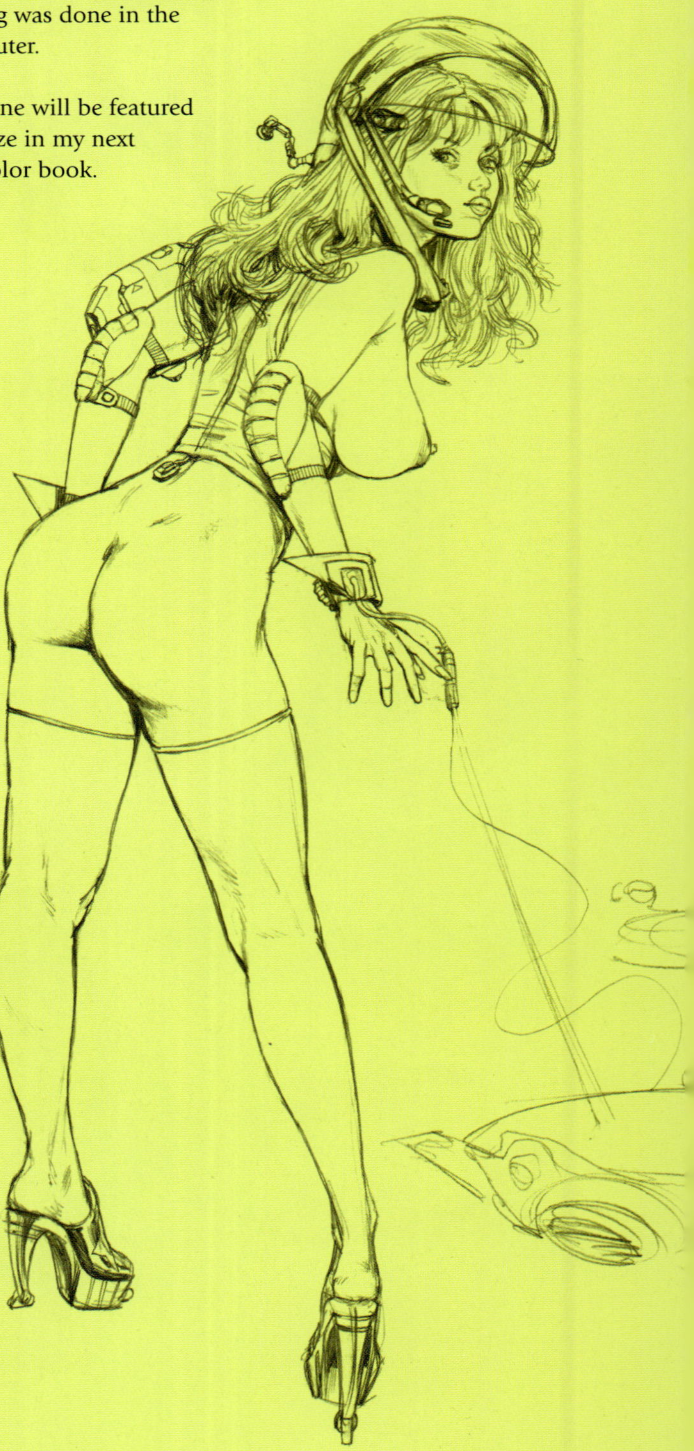

Pet a Porter –
Skateboard fashion meets
Bugs Bunny, with a tethered,
floating suitcase
rack that reminds
me of K-9 from
Doctor Who.
I really enjoyed
laying out this
page as a tribute
to 1940s' Cheesecake
artists.

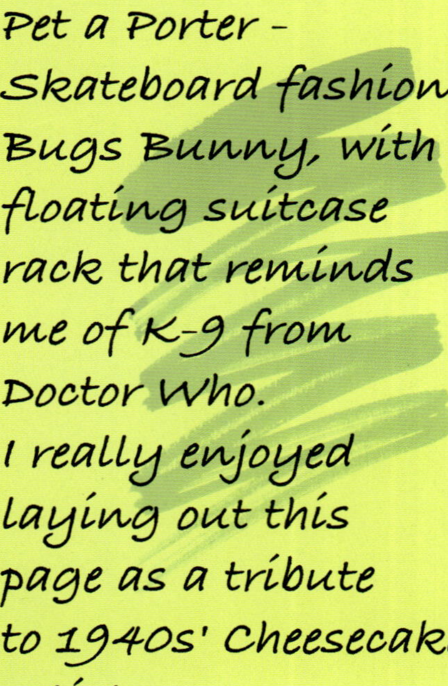

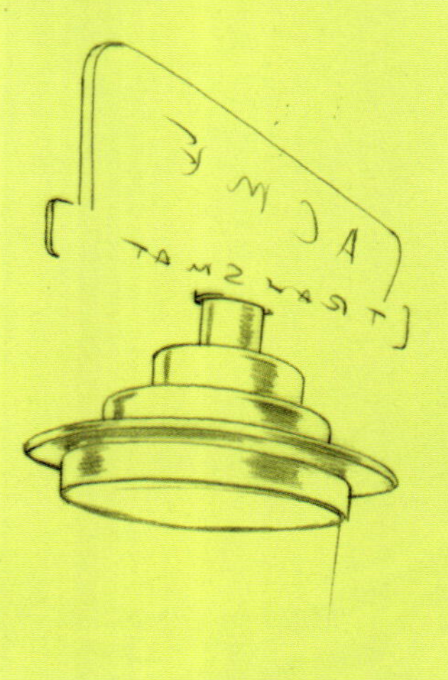

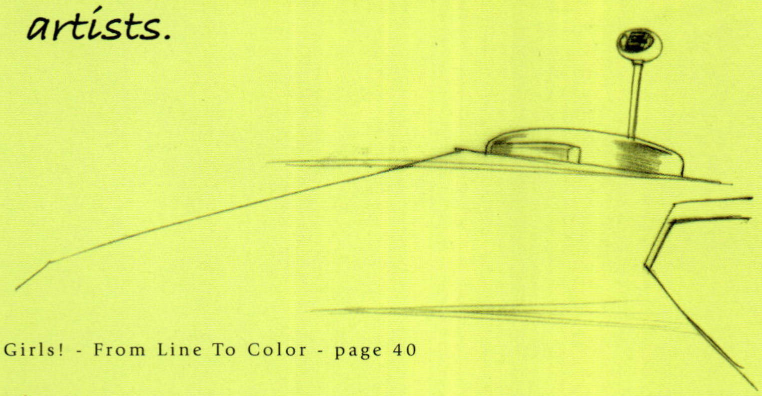

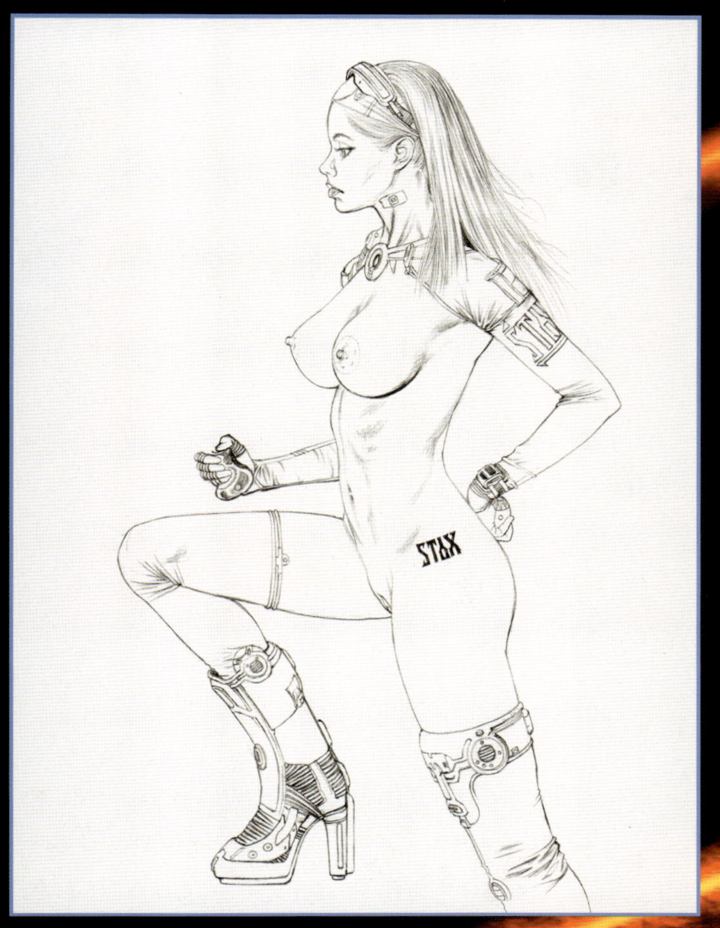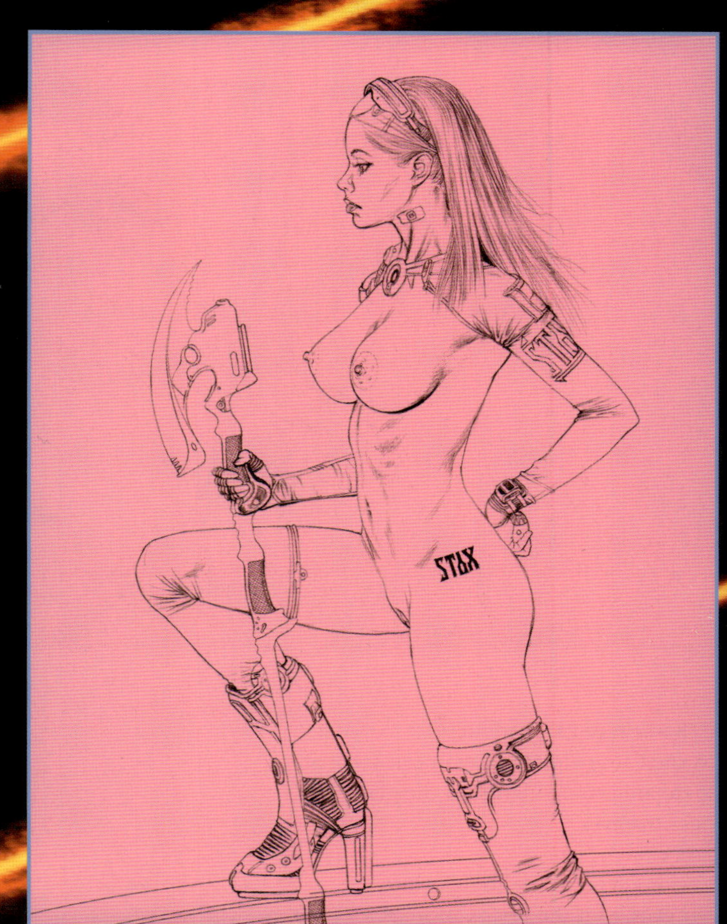

0098-Spacegirl Step Up - this piece was from my first book, *Girl Crazy - The Art of Michal Dutkiewicz*. I kept the work-up to a minimum in some areas, to help keep it strong and effective. One of my favorites, again. Unfortunately I didn't save more step-by-step from this piece.

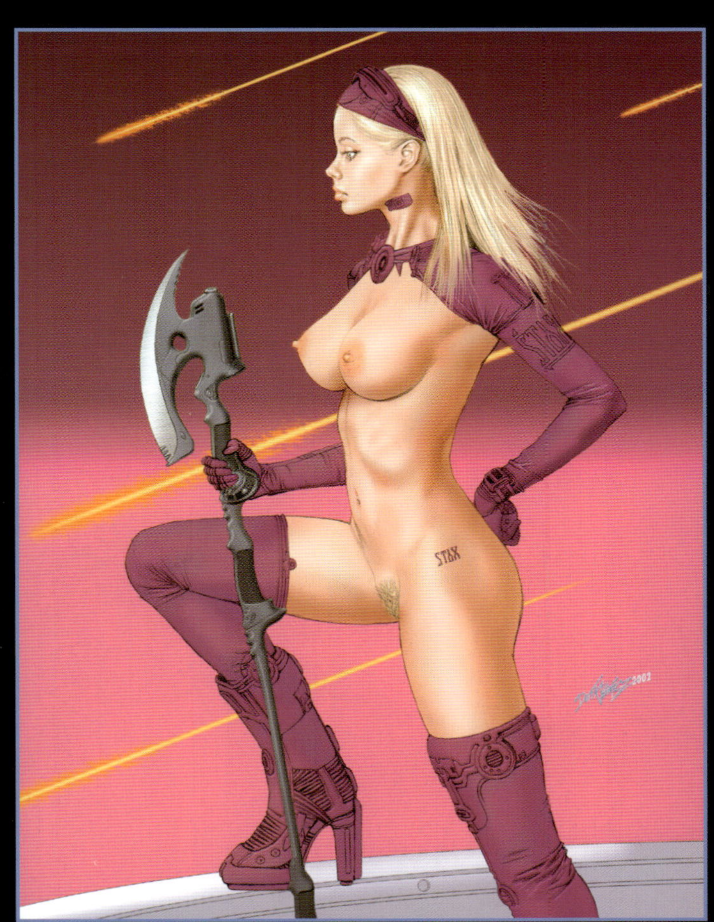

Inspired by Jaime Pressly, Travis Charest and Black & Decker power tools, but modeled on about 10 different photographs. For once, I restrained the size of the bust on my figure. I am often criticized for the gargantuan size of breasts in my pictures, because guys keep telling me how gross large breasts are - AWWW!

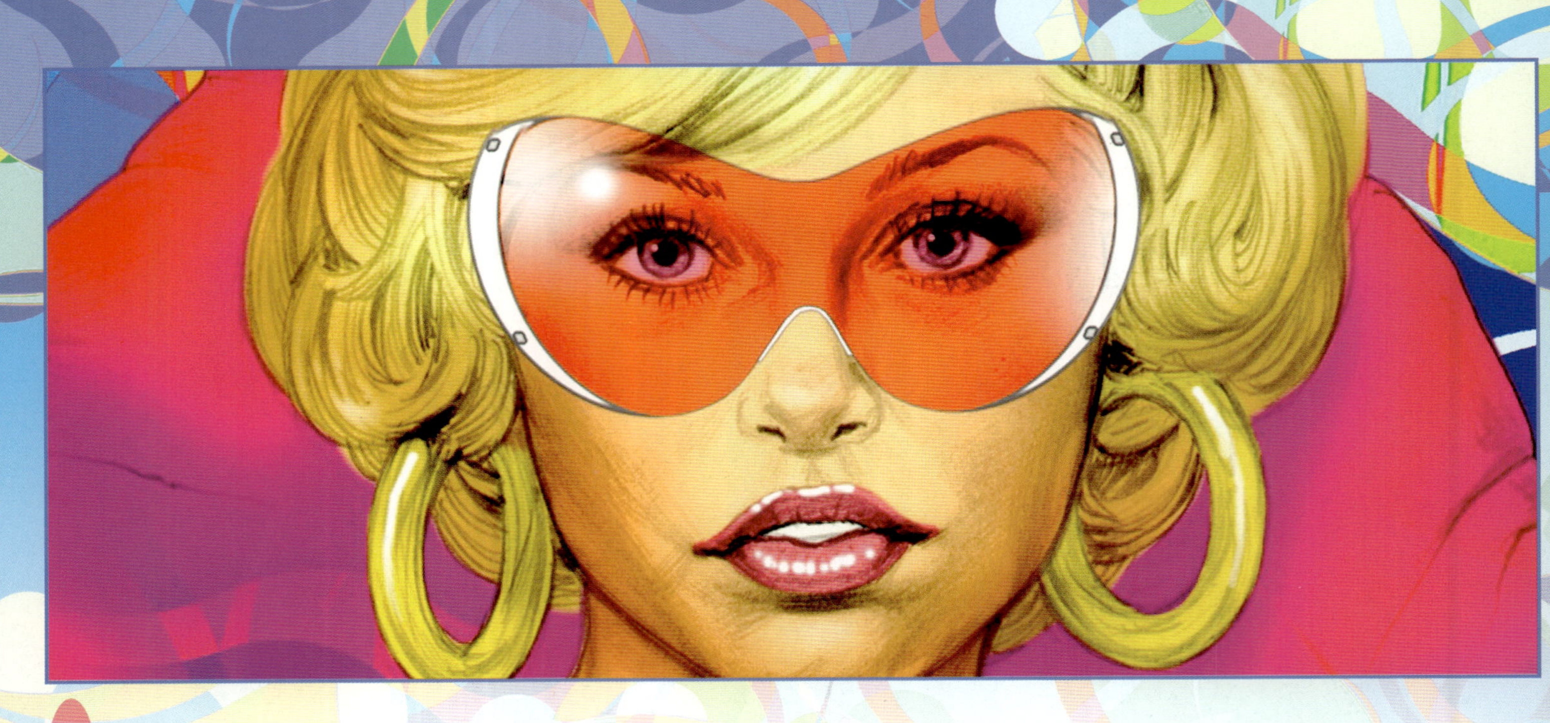

0284-Brassy Psychedelic.
In the Close-Up above, you can see that there are no highlights on the glasses near the eyes.

I wanted you to see straight into her eyes, as if the Rose-Colored Lenses give her a naive, optimistic quality - a bit like the way people were before the greed and selfishness, which have been espoused as virtues in more recent times, took over.

The pose for this picture was like a 'Gift-From-God' - I was websurfing and I came across a girl called Evelyn Lory who had a wonderful Posing Style... ...Instead of the usual hours of research and comparison, it was perfect and fitted exactly with the rough sketch I had done...

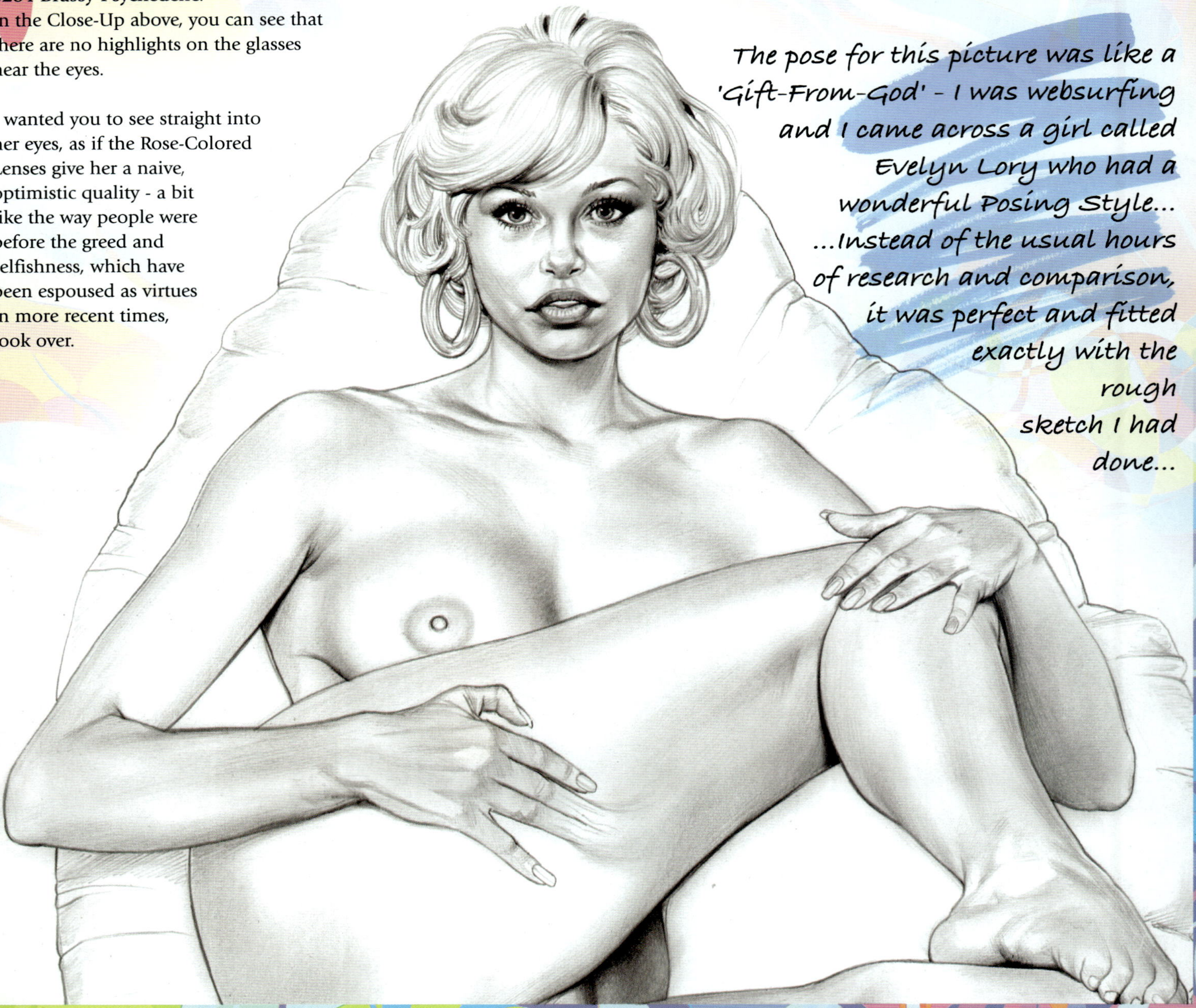

... The background was inspired by the paintings of Bruce Vinall, as well as those of my brother, Adam, who is an Art Historian and Writer, as well as a great Abstract Painter. We both started as Abstract Painters, but once I got bitten by illustration, I realized this was something I could really sink my teeth into.

The pattern, however, is based on Hot Rod and Biker Flame Patterns - what a fusion!

The glasses are drawn from a real item from Dior.

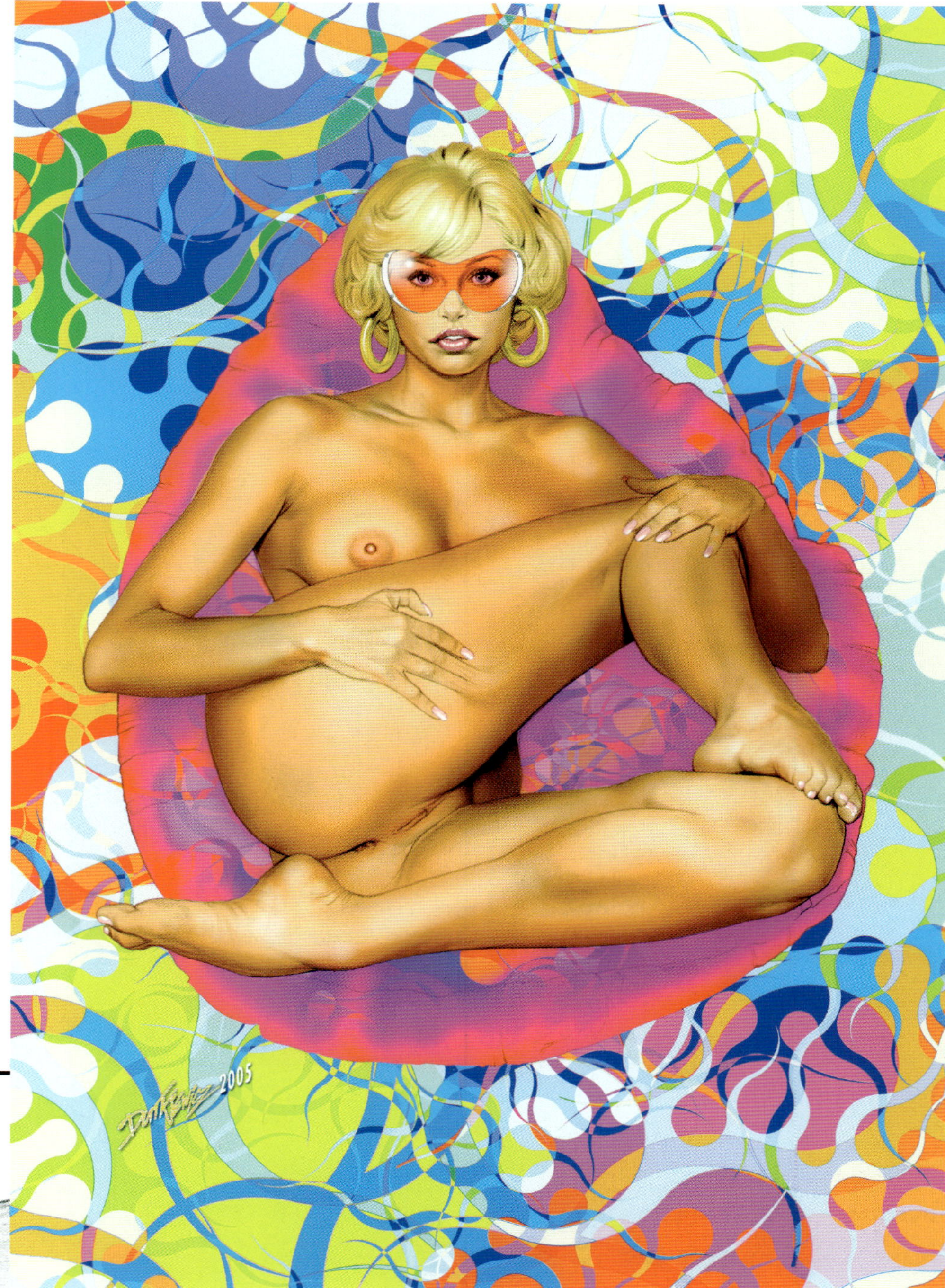

At Left - the fingers disappearing into the leg may seem macabre or sinister, but it was a way of referring to the rather fluid nature of reality in the late 1960s and early '70s.

Also, the fingers seemed to be too 'much' for the composition.

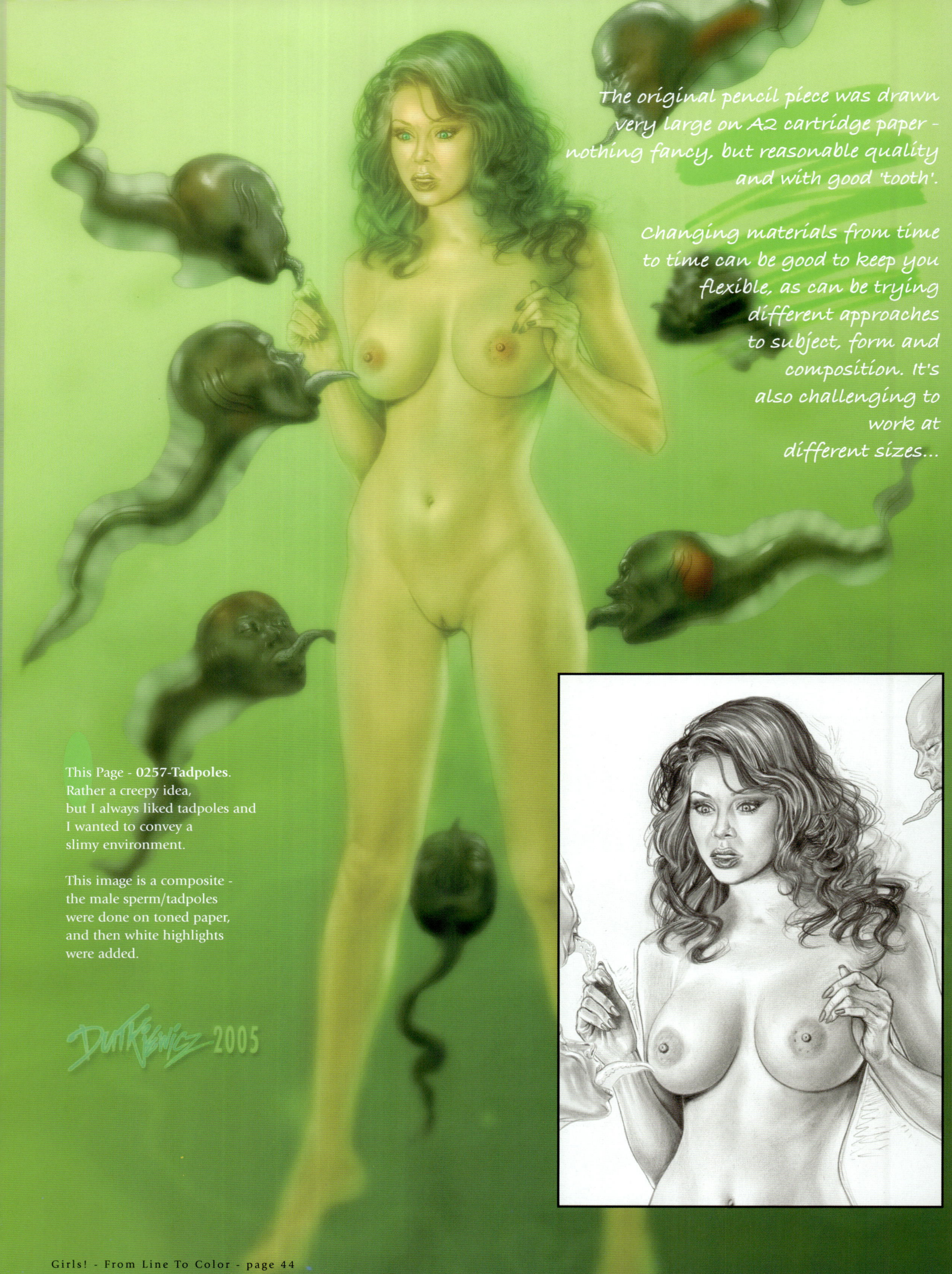

This Page - **0257-Tadpoles**.
Rather a creepy idea,
but I always liked tadpoles and
I wanted to convey a
slimy environment.

This image is a composite -
the male sperm/tadpoles
were done on toned paper,
and then white highlights
were added.

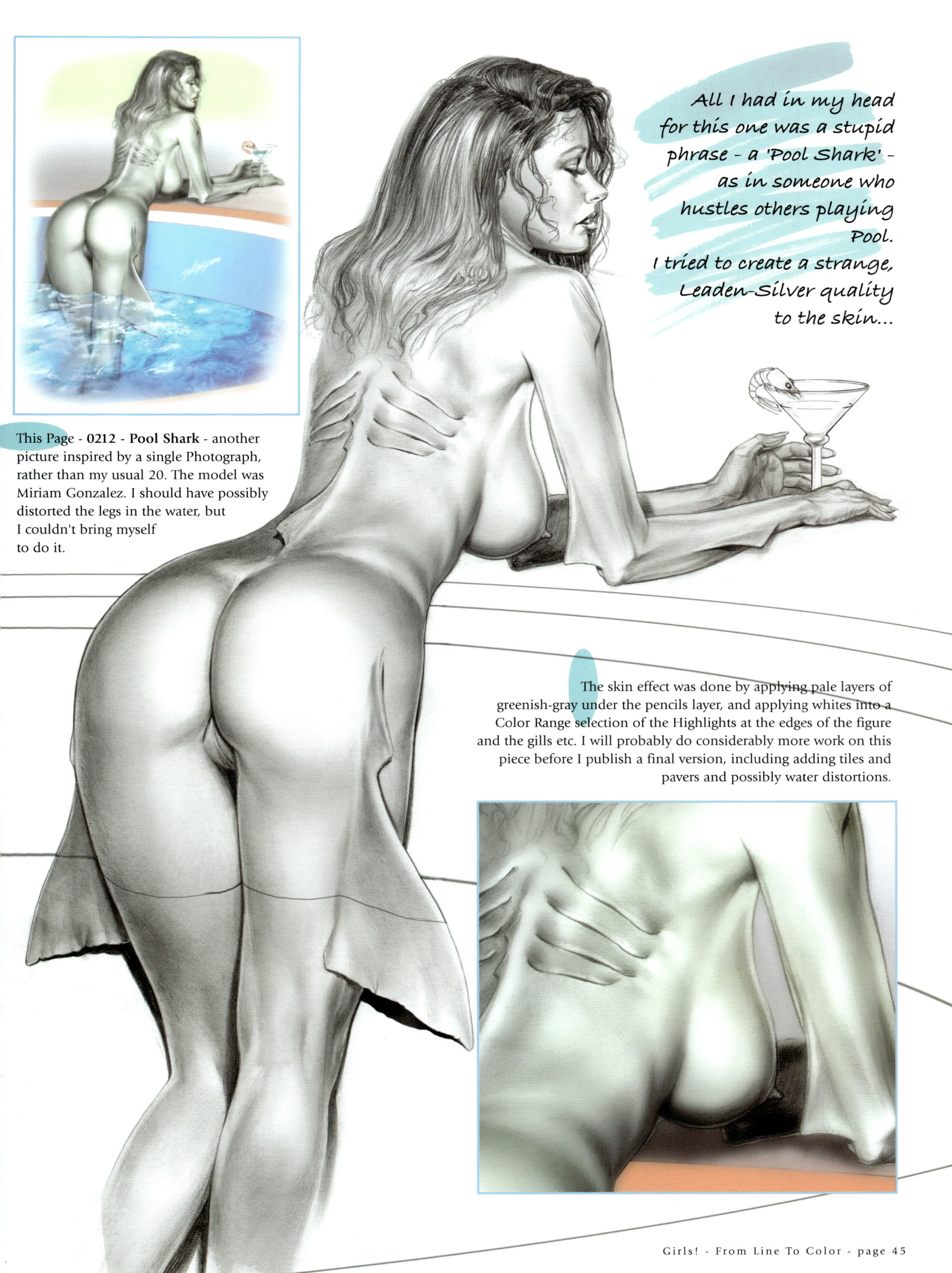

This Page - **0212** - **Pool Shark** - another picture inspired by a single Photograph, rather than my usual 20. The model was Miriam Gonzalez. I should have possibly distorted the legs in the water, but I couldn't bring myself to do it.

The skin effect was done by applying pale layers of greenish-gray under the pencils layer, and applying whites into a Color Range selection of the Highlights at the edges of the figure and the gills etc. I will probably do considerably more work on this piece before I publish a final version, including adding tiles and pavers and possibly water distortions.

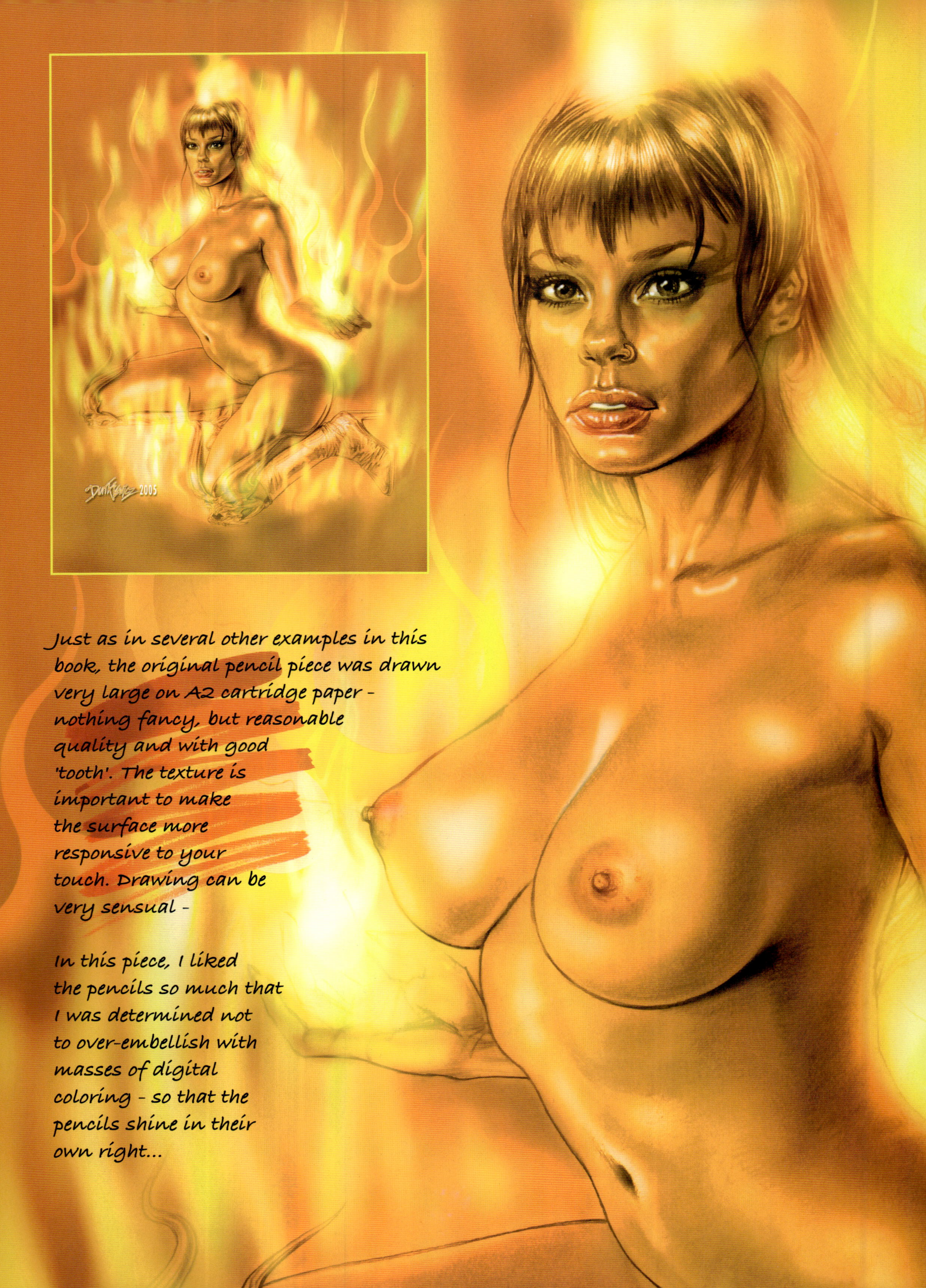

Just as in several other examples in this book, the original pencil piece was drawn very large on A2 cartridge paper - nothing fancy, but reasonable quality and with good 'tooth'. The texture is important to make the surface more responsive to your touch. Drawing can be very sensual -

In this piece, I liked the pencils so much that I was determined not to over-embellish with masses of digital coloring - so that the pencils shine in their own right...

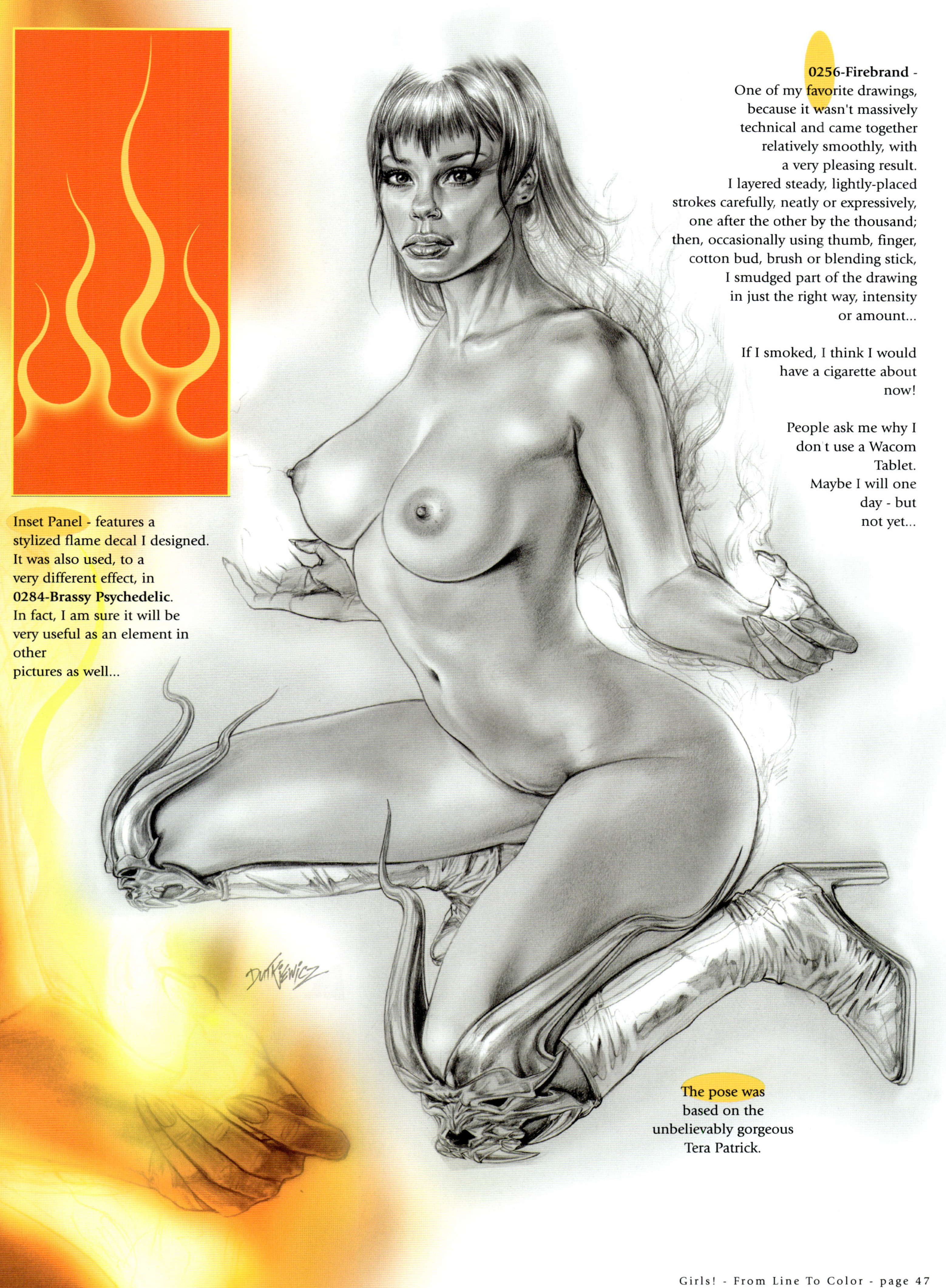

0256-Firebrand -
One of my favorite drawings,
because it wasn't massively
technical and came together
relatively smoothly, with
a very pleasing result.
I layered steady, lightly-placed
strokes carefully, neatly or expressively,
one after the other by the thousand;
then, occasionally using thumb, finger,
cotton bud, brush or blending stick,
I smudged part of the drawing
in just the right way, intensity
or amount...

If I smoked, I think I would
have a cigarette about
now!

People ask me why I
don t use a Wacom
Tablet.
Maybe I will one
day - but
not yet...

Inset Panel - features a
stylized flame decal I designed.
It was also used, to a
very different effect, in
0284-Brassy Psychedelic.
In fact, I am sure it will be
very useful as an element in
other
pictures as well...

The pose was
based on the
unbelievably gorgeous
Tera Patrick.

This was a quick pencil piece with a
minimal amount of computer coloring. The Highlights were
also done in pencil. It was used in Picture Magazine.
Sometimes a piece shows potential for further
development. I always get a kick
out of looking at this one, so maybe you will see
a more elaborate version in my next
full-color book.

NTRAL PARK

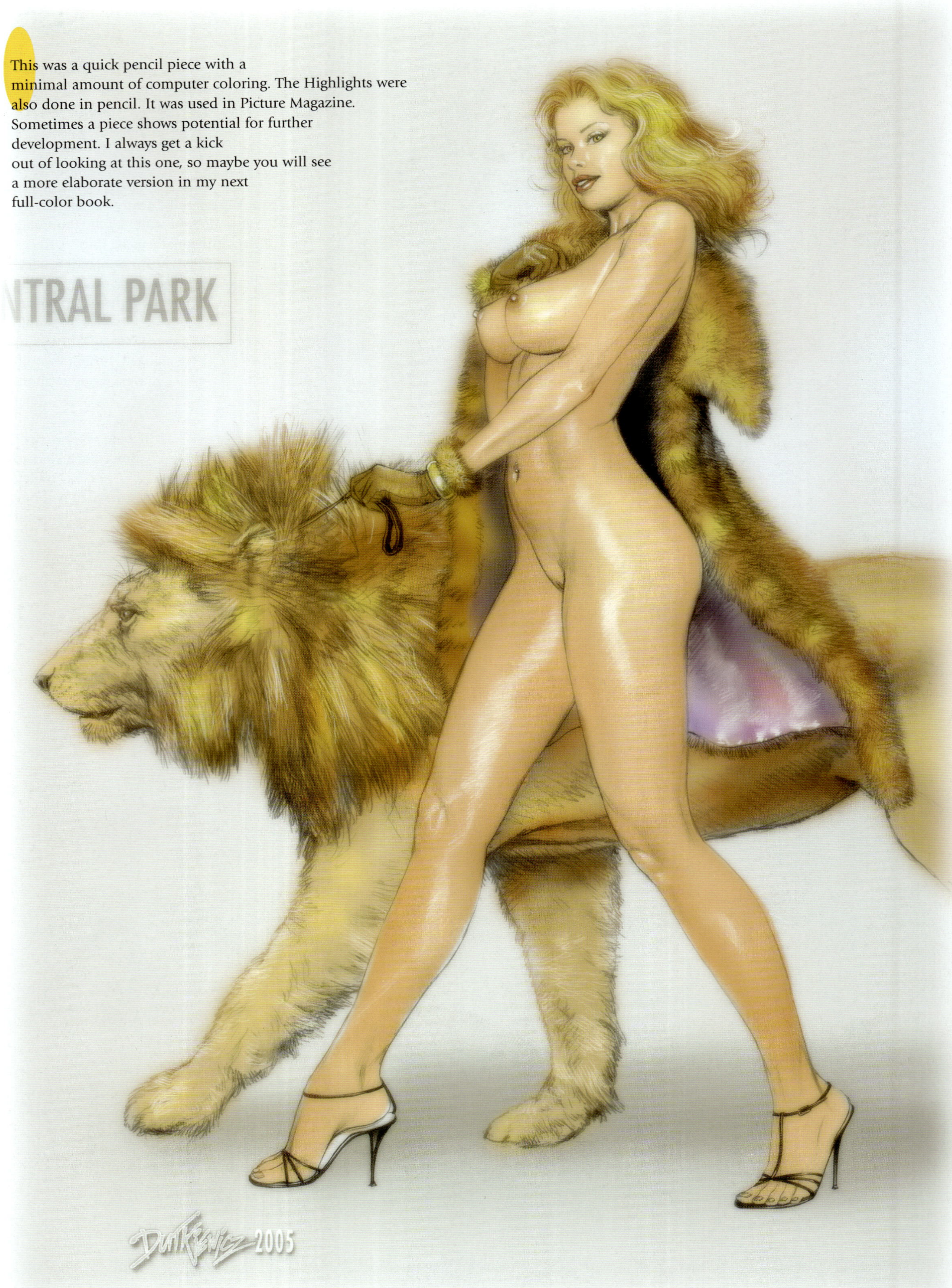